Swimming in Circles is Better Than Drowning

Leanne Garrett Flanagan

authorHOUSE®

AuthorHouse™
1663 Liberty Drive
Bloomington, IN 47403
www.authorhouse.com
Phone: 1-800-839-8640

First published by AuthorHouse 8/15/2011

ISBN: 978-1-4634-0423-9 (e)
ISBN: 978-1-4634-0424-6 (sc)

Library of Congress Control Number: 2011908654

Printed in the United States of America

To live content with small means, to seek elegance rather than luxury, and refinement rather than fashion; study hard, think quietly, talk gently, act frankly; to listen to starts and birds, to babes and sages, with open heart; to bear all cheerfully, do all bravely, await occasions, hurry never. In a word, to let the spiritual, unbidden and unconscious, grow up through the common. This is to be my symphony.

--William Henry Channing

To Rob, my love and best friend--
For your encouragement, indulgence and
support of all my creative endeavors.

Introduction

Being "DADDY'S LITTLE GIRL" IN the '50's, I lived for a time in a sheltered, pink, sugar coated world. My family lived what was considered in those years, the "American Dream". After graduation from high school, I went to college in a time when most women chose to attend with hopes of finding a suitable career until they married and had a family. A suitable career usually meant one as a teacher, nurse, or secretary. More importantly, for some women attending college in the mid 60's, education was secondary to finding a husband, living happily ever after with 2.5 children, a house in the suburbs with a Betty Crocker kitchen and a Stepford Wives mentality (although the Stepford Wives was not to be aired as a dogma for many years).

I followed the prototype and married soon after graduating from a 2-year college program with a major in Secretarial Science (there was nothing scientific about it). Family life fulfilled my being for many years. I faithfully tried to keep up with the Baby Boomer Manual for women. Oh, you didn't get one of those? Life was good.

As I attained my dutifuldaughter/wonderwife/supermom/careerwomen status, I slowly realized this was not working for me. I then started to choose my own special way to emotionally cope with situations thrown at me that complicated my life, like rocks flying into a lawnmower, which would, as you can imagine, complicate mowing the front lawn. What followed were some difficult times. I share those with you in this book in essays and poems, both serious and light.

As I move forward into the Golden Years, I see longevity being thrown at me whether I want it or not (and I am not entirely sure that I do---want it, that is). Through the miracle of modern medicine and technology, doctors replace body parts like mechanics replace parts of a car. Yet it is very often difficult to get another human being on the other end of the telephone! Somehow, that seems rather twisted to me.

Although writing has become my favorite pastime, it has also played an extremely important role in the recovery of a person who was once lost within herself. The inherent destructive tendencies fed by an even more destructive substance made a lethal combination for me. I am very grateful that I live during a time when I am afforded the chance to receive excellent, safe treatment that helped me transition to a happier, more productive woman.

This book is my way of sharing experiences, renewed strength and new hope with you. Along with that, I hope you also get a few laughs, reflect a bit on the sometimes unexpected, sometimes wonderful, at times unfair and often extraordinary twists and turns that life throws us. Perhaps you will also find a few words that bring back a memory or two from your journey in time.

Table of Contents

Those
Fabulous
Fifties

Thoughts of Home

IN 1952, MY PARENTS BOUGHT a four-acre estate complete with a large run-down house, barn, chicken coop, apple orchard, areas of rocky hills and overgrown woods. It was to become a lovely home for our family after extensive renovations. The '50s were a prosperous time for my parents. They were most likely very excited by the project they undertook. As a little baby boomer, growing up in what at that time was upper middle class, this family is what shaped my view of the world and my future.

I was four years old when we moved into our new home in northern New Jersey. My brother was ten. Our new home included four acres of land and, being an outdoor kind of guy, my brother was thrilled to have all of that space to play. Since I was a little girl who frequently lived in my own dream world, I quickly scouted out secret play houses and hideaways in the side yards.

Mom and Dad took painstaking care in their monumental renovation project. With great intensity and focus, as was my mother's nature, they conducted an exhaustive search for the best contractors and craftsmen. As vice president of the North Atlantic and Gulf Steamship Company in New York City, Dad could now afford this undertaking. Mom had given up her secretarial position to raise a family. Now the struggling seemed to be over for them. Dad had reached his goal as an executive. He had a beautifully furnished corner office overlooking the East River.

I remember many workmen being at the house for a long time. The small windows along the east side of the living room were replaced with contemporary six-foot-long windows. These expansive new windows opened up that entire side of our house, giving us a spectacular view of a rock garden which my mother designed and planted. Although we had a landscaper and gardener to care for the rest of the grounds, this area was "hands-off" to the professionals. The rocky hillside garden was Mom's special piece that brought her peace. Beyond the rock garden was about an acre of undeveloped hilly, rocky terrain bordered by wooded areas. While we lived there, the acreage bordering that land remained undeveloped. It protected us from the main road (a two-lane highway at that time) which lay about 100 feet below.

The "lower forty," as my father jokingly called the half acre near the road on the other side of the property, was an open field of wild bushes and beautiful wild flowers growing along the main road. Next to the "lower forty"

was the beginning of our winding one-quarter-mile, long, single lane driveway. The biggest challenge of Dad's workday was timing his departure for the train station so that he and the bread delivery man or milk man would not collide head on in the middle of the driveway. If they met at all, Dad would need to back up to the house again since the delivery man could not back out into the busy main road. Recalling what I have been told of my father's sense of humor, I imagine some bets were made among the three men about the number of times this happened during a one year period.

I do not remember how long it took to renovate the house and make it a home. I vividly remember, however, the man who handcrafted and installed built-in window seats under the long picture windows on the side of our living room. Mr. Olsen was from Denmark. He came to work in the early morning in his old wood-trimmed Ford station wagon with his favorite companion, his Great Dane, Thor. He ate his breakfast in the car, refusing my mother's invitation to sit in the house with us. He then began work with the dog, and me, at his side. When the dog sat next to me, he was as tall as I was when standing. One day, while Thor and I were quietly watching Mr. Olsen work, Thor turned and licked my face from chin to forehead with one swift, sweeping slurp of his giant tongue. I was astonished by this sudden gesture of love. My face must have shown it (I probably turned beet red), because Mr. Olsen burst into laughter. Sometimes, he told stories about his family and "the old country," but mostly we were silent, he busy with his work and I a fascinated onlooker. Later, I would spend a great deal of time on those window seats, looking out at the garden, the changing seasons and the animals that visited our yard. It was a wonderful spot for daydreaming.

The rest of the living room was also completely redone in the latest '50s style. All of the moldings were handcrafted. Moldings, window seat and furniture were all blond wood, the latest trend in home design. Mr. Olsen also built a curved desk into the wall in an alcove off the main living room. Our piano stood on the wall opposite the desk. There Mom and I spent many hours. There was even a Picasso-style oil painting, displayed above the piano. It was a piece of modern art which was so popular at that time; my mother kept it until she died.

In the living room, a black coffee table was custom built to complement the curve of the pumpkin-colored, nubbin couch. Two overstuffed chairs in a modern brown and beige print with pumpkin accents, were placed on one side of the couch. Across the room on the other side of the couch were two low-slung, brown tweed chairs. Those chairs became my favorite TV seats. They were a perfect fit for me. Too close, of course, to the TV, as my mother always scolded.

Opposite the pumpkin couch was a magnificent stone wall with a fireplace. My brother recalls that dad had the mason buy Tennessee stone and hand cut it for our fireplace. It was cut by hand because it was too thick to cut by any machine made in the '50s. On one side of the fireplace was the door leading to our screened-in back porch where we had more casual summer meals. Dad, being a creative creature of comfort, had our carpenter, Mike, build a turnstile on the other side of the fireplace. A platform on the turnstile held our television set. In the summer, we would turn the platform around to the porch so that my dad and brother could watch ballgames there. As a family, we also watched other favorites of the times; *The Texaco Hour* with Milton Berle and the *Ed Sullivan Show*. No mosquitoes; we had screens! The only sounds in the quiet, cool summer evenings were the crickets.

My brother and I spent many days fighting over who would watch the favorite children's shows on TV. . . *Lone Ranger, Gene Autry, Roy Rogers,* or *Superman* for him. I liked *Miss Frances's Ding Dong School* and *Howdy Dowdy Time*. At about age nine, my all-time favorite was Walt Disney's *Mickey Mouse Club*, starring the Mouseketeers. The world got put on hold daily at four o'clock when that show came on. Anything else I might have been doing stopped. I remember idolizing all of the preteen Mouseketeers. I wanted so much to become one of them; I loved to perform. My first love was dancing and singing. A large part of my week was spent at dancing and music lessons with many practice sessions. I had great confidence that I could easily pass an audition to be a Mouseketeer. I envisioned myself with the ears on my blonde head, smiling as I introduced myself to the zillions of fans watching every day at four p.m. Then, Bobby and I, dressed in wonderful costumes, would sing and dance. There would be lots of letters from fans all over America. I even begged my parents to move to California so that I too could be on TV with Annette, Darlene, Cubby, Karen, Bobby and

the rest of the gang. I was absolutely devastated and truly did not understand when they attempted to explain that such a move was impossible for us.

Because my parents were members of the Country Club set, they held many dinners and cocktail parties in our home. I often stood at the top of the stairway, looking down into the living room. I was mesmerized by the ladies in their elegant cocktail dresses with form-fitting bodices and crinoline-supported skirts. Most had a martini glass in one hand and a cigarette in the other. There was a great deal of noisy conversation and laughter. The background music came from our new stereophonic record player. Evenings usually began with couples conversing in groups. Slowly, the ladies and men would ultimately drift apart: men discussing business, woman their clubs, charities, new recipes and children. At the end of the cocktail hour, the party would move on to a restaurant or perhaps to New York for dinner and a Broadway show. After the party moved on, I sometimes wandered downstairs amid the empty cocktail glasses and dirty ashtrays, sat on the couch and pretended that I, too, wore a party dress and held a martini and a cigarette. I had imaginary conversations with another sophisticated lady or gentleman. Breaking the spell, Grandma ultimately caught me and sent me back upstairs to bed.

Our maternal grandmother lived with us. She had her own room in her own private part of our house off the hallway from the kitchen. She was a very serious person; I don't remember her smiling often. She emigrated from Germany to this country as a child and lived through the Depression, raising six children. Now that she had a lovely family who all lived nearby with their children, I often wondered why she looked so stern most of the time. I do think she believed my mother and father spoiled us. Grandma took care of my brother and me when Mom and Dad went out. We asked Mom to cook for us before she left because Grandma only cooked two ways, overcooked or undercooked. Her hamburgers always ended up like hockey pucks, her spaghetti, crunchy. If Grandma cooked for us, we usually fed it to the dog.

Our family lived in this house for seven years until 1959. A short, sudden illness took my father's life at age forty-six. Our world was turned suddenly, tragically upside down. I was no longer daddy's little girl. My brother was to face his late teen years without his dad. My mother was forced to sell our home and return to work as a secretary after twenty years of homemaking. Being eleven years old, I did not grasp the magnitude of my mother's loss, shock and desolation. When we moved from our wonderful home to the top floor of a two-family home in a new town, I only remember feeling frightened and lonely. It was summertime. My mom would be going back to work. I would have to stay home by myself. I knew no one. I would be starting the seventh grade, so I was full of anxiety about whether I would make friends and fit in with the kids. The new town was very unlike where I came from. I jokingly refer to those years in my childhood home as "The Princess in the Ivory Tower House" years. I was now entering another world – which turned out to be a good one, just different.

A few years after the house was sold, we found out it was sold again to a developer who razed the house and constructed a medical office building with lots and lots of parking.

I know my memories dwell in a place that no longer exists. The home my parents lovingly created, which I once thought would be there forever, was gone, crushed into dust. It illustrated what we all realize as we grow into adulthood; how fragile what we have is on any given day.

The Train Station

My brother and I are called in from play,
We have to fetch Dad from the station.
We're allowed a book or toy for the car,
But the waiting is an abomination!

The trains all chug by us, slow down to a stop,
men in suits getting off one by one.
Off the train, down the steps, tired faces we see;
happy homecoming, workday is done.

Mom, brother and I search the crowd high and low.
"On the next one," mom says with good cheer.
Ten more minutes pass by, the next train pulls in.
Oh please, God, let our dad be here!

As the 5:45 slowly rolls from the station,
we see a familiar sight.
Our dad is asleep in the third row back,
missed his stop yet again tonight!

Home we drive, hungry now, stony silence prevails.
Mom is mad at Dad's napping. we know.
He'll be taking a cab home, arrive very late
and for dinner be eating crow.

Rules of the Day

April, 1959

I<small>T SEEMS AS IF</small> M<small>OMMY</small> has been talking to the lady at the hospital desk for an awfully long time. She is trying to tell her to please let me go see my daddy who is very sick on the third floor. I have not seen him in eight days. He was brought to the hospital last week when he fell down walking to his car at the train station, on his way home from working in New York at the North Atlantic and Gulf Steamship Company where he is the Vice President. Sometimes he takes me there and lets me sit at his big desk in his office. He has a chair that spins around and around. His secretary, who is a very nice lady, gets me soda and cookies and lets me have paper and pencils to draw with. I love looking at all the big ships in the East River. I like Uncle Ralph and Uncle John who Daddy works with.

They always tell me how cute I am and tell me jokes and make me laugh. Then Daddy and I get to come home on the train together.

Anyway, I wonder what is taking Mommy so long. I think she is crying now. She has been crying a lot this week. It makes me sad to see her crying so much. My big brother Curt is very sad too. He is seventeen and has lots of girlfriends, but I don't really like any of them much, except for Susan; she's nice. He yells at me if I'm not nice to his friends. He makes me practice dancing with him so he can dance really well with the girls. I have fun doing that.

No one will tell me what's wrong with Daddy. They think I am too little, but I am not, I am old enough to know. I am his little girl after all.

I hear Mommy saying to the lady at the desk, "You don't understand, my husband is critically ill. He needs to see his daughter! If we wait, it may be . . ." and then she is crying again and I can't understand the rest. The hospital has this rule that children are not allowed to see the sick people because they think children have too many germs. You have to be older to see the sick people, even if they are your father. I think this is a silly rule.

Then my aunt Edie comes in and makes my mommy sit down on a chair next to me. "Mommy, please don't cry," I said. But she can't help it. My aunt talks some more to the lady and asks her to call the doctor and get permission for me to go upstairs to the third floor to see my daddy.

15

The lady says, "No, I cannot do that. It is against hospital policy to have a child visit a patient."

"Well," my aunt says, "this is a very extenuating circumstance. Can't she just go up for a few moments? She is very well behaved and won't cause any problems."

The lady goes to talk to another lady with a different badge on. Aunt Edie turns around and smiles at Mommy like she is thinking maybe they are going to let me upstairs to the third floor to see my daddy. Then the lady with the different badge comes over to Mommy and leans over her and says, "I'm terribly sorry, dear, but we cannot allow your little girl upstairs. We have a very strict rule here about allowing children to see patients."

"But please," my mommy says, "she loves her daddy so much." But the lady is walking away. Now my mommy has to go upstairs to see my daddy, so I stay with my aunt. I start to cry too because I really miss him and I think if I could give him a kiss and sing a song for him, he might feel better. After all, I'm not sick. Not even a sniffle. I know that we all have germs but since I am not sick at all, how could I have any bad germs that might hurt Daddy?

I don't get to see my daddy that day.

2002

When my granddaughter was born in 2002, her older sister, age four was welcomed as a visitor to the maternity floor of the large hospital where her mother had given birth.

My, my how things change over the years. The advances in modern medicine are truly patient-friendly. I just never realized that the intensity of germs that children carry has lessened over the years.

April 17, 1959

I SUDDENLY FEEL MY SHOULDER BEING shaken gently, and a voice calling me that I only vaguely recognize saying "Leanne, you have to come downstairs, your mother wants you." I am a little annoyed; I was enjoying a lovely dream. I look up to see my cousin, Dorothy, who is about twenty-one years old at the time, and I think, "Why in the world she is here so late at night? Is something wrong? Are my other cousins, her younger sister Jane, my age, here to play?" We usually only see each other for summer vacations, picnics and holidays.

I think," No, I must still be asleep and my dream just changed over to a different one."

But Dorothy has a serious look on her face and sounds upset. I can see she has been crying. I am getting scared. Then I start to think that maybe my daddy is not any better.

"What's the matter?" I whine. "Is my daddy okay?"

"Just come on now. Put your robe and slippers on, and come downstairs," she pushed gently.

I start to run down the stairs. When I get to the bottom and look up, there is a confusing, eerie scene before me: my living room, full of people – my grandmother, aunts, uncles and friends of my mother and father, all looking at me and some are crying. Then they turn their heads to a chair near the couch and I see a small figure in the chair, hands over her face, bent over, sobbing as if her heart is broken. It's my mommy and her heart is broken.

She looks up when she hears me and says, "Oh honey, Daddy died!"

I don't know what to do. Someone leads me to the pumpkin-colored kidney-shaped deco couch to sit by another cousin and I start to cry. I sit on that couch listening to all the grown-ups whispering about what a shame it is, how he was too young to die; how maybe if he managed his diabetes better; how it is too bad he left such a beautiful, young family. They wonder what Marie will do now, did he have a lot of insurance? Did he leave her with enough so she won't have to work? After all, she hasn't worked in twenty years and jobs have changed. On and on they talk and it's all becoming like one long never-ending note from a song we sing in chorus. After hearing all these well-meaning people all I can think of through my dried up tears is, "What will we do without him, how will we live? We won't have enough money." That's me, practical little Virgo that I am. I am starting to get sleepy now. Do I have to listen anymore? Can't I sit with mommy? My brother, who is seventeen now, is in our kitchen. My cousin tells me some friends of my dad are trying to calm him down because besides being sad, he seems to be really mad about dad dying and leaving us alone.

After awhile I just feel quiet and really sad so I just stare straight ahead. I don't want to talk to anybody. I guess I feel kind of numb. Then I get up off the couch to go over to give my mommy a hug. She hugs me back, but she starts to cry again. My favorite aunt brings me upstairs and sits with me awhile, hugging me and stroking my hair, telling me that everything will be all right. I think she is wrong, even though I know she is just trying to be nice. Nothing will ever be all right again. I miss my dad already. I do not understand. How could God take away my daddy? I guess God really wanted him. That's what we learned in Sunday School about people who die. God wants them with him.

I overhear funeral services being planned by someone, probably not by mommy, since she doesn't seem to be able to stop crying. No family member or anyone close to me has ever died before, so I sit for two awful days they call the "wake" (My daddy just died. I really want to ask someone why this is called "wake," but I am too embarrassed). I watch between one and two hundred people line up to view the body of my daddy and trying to make mommy feel better. I saw her taking some kind of pills today. My brother told me it is to help her stay calm through the funeral so she can greet all the people who came to see her and say they are sorry daddy died.

I cannot go into the viewing room at the funeral home although mommy tries to coax me to come in, saying, "It's all right, you don't have to be scared, honey, come here and sit next to me." I just can't go close to daddy lying there in a suit not moving. It is just awful. He doesn't move. It doesn't seem like he is really daddy. I don't want to go near him. I will stay away. Then he won't really be dead to me. A few of my cousins are at the funeral home. I mostly sit with them in another room until we go home to eat and then come back here for a few more hours. It will be over tomorrow.

They told me that daddy was cremated, but our family did not go to the crematorium. I don't know what that means, but I don't really care. Our minister made a speech and said how good daddy was and mommy cried more and so did a lot of other people. I watched everybody and cried some more too. Even my brother cried and I never saw him cry but I know he is very sad too. We really like our minister, Mr. Van. Mom, my brother and I go to church each week. She tells us all of the time that Dad did not think he needed a Sunday service. He tried to act as a good Christian all the time so in his mind, this was all God required of him and he preferred to rest on Sunday. She also told us this was a matter they often disagreed on, but that they still loved each other very much. After the funeral service, Mr. Van went over to talk to mom and my brother for a very long time. Then many, many people come back to our house after the service to eat and drink a lot. I don't know why. One minute they are sad and now the grown-ups all want to be with us and have a party.

Why is that? I am still wondering what is going to happen to us, if my mom is ever going to be happy again, and if my brother is ever going to act like himself again.

My mother does not seem like she wants to have this party. Neither do I.

Mother of Mine

MARIE WAS A PETITE, ADORABLE brunette who, I am told, had a sweet, lovable personality and was fun to be with. She was the youngest of six children, born to a German immigrant grocer, Henry and his wife, Ellen. Marie graduated from high school, which was not always the case during the Depression years and she landed a secretarial position in New York City where the only big businesses were located back then. She soon married her high school sweetheart who was ambitiously working his way up, literally, from the mailroom of a shipping business. He was a real charmer, I am also told by many. He had studied for a short while at the University of Virginia, but it was rumored that he left when my grandfather ran out of money because of the hard economic times. Not allowing this to curb his ambition, he took his wit, charm and sense of humor along with his intelligence to NewYork City and the shipping business.

While Mom and Dad were in high school, Dad was the class president and Mom was his sweetheart. They remained sweethearts and married in 1936. During World War II, my father was enlisted to work for the government with the ships that brought supplies to our troops, an important job that fortunately kept him in the States. My brother was born in the spring of 1941 outside of Chicago, where Dad was working for the war effort. After the war, he started working for another steamship company in New York City and remained there for many years.

Mom, Dad and my brother lived with my grandparents in Ridgefield Park, New Jersey, where my parents had grown up. I was born in 1947. A few years later, we moved further west into the suburbs, wanting more space. We moved several times; evidently, Mom was unhappy with one thing or another; neighbors, shops, schoolteachers. They finally settled in our large home on the hill when I was four. Life was good until 1957, when Dad was diagnosed with diabetes. In 1957, treatments were not as advanced as those available today. He immediately started injections of insulin several times a day, but there seemed to be a problem controlling the disease in his case. In the spring of 1959, he collapsed at the train station one day, was hospitalized and died about ten days later.

After my father's death, Mom had to sell our home and we moved to the top floor of a two-family house in a small town in northern New Jersey. After twenty years of being a homemaker, Mom sharpened her secretarial skills and her courage, landing a job in a large engineering firm which handled government contracts. Along with the normal qualifications for a secretarial position, she had to have a complete background check by the Federal Government, which included her complete public service background, namely her years of Brownie Troop leadership and PTA service. Since she had no dark secrets and had not led a double life, she passed their scrutiny. Because of her excellent job performance and dedication, she went from the typing pool to secretary to the Chief Engineer in a short time. Unfortunately, Mom did not heal emotionally from the loss of my father as quickly. I remember that for a few years, she did make friends with co-workers and occasionally went out for an evening with girlfriends, but that was short-lived.

Gradually, she isolated herself more and more. She came home from work, we ate dinner, I did homework, and then we watched TV and went to bed. I doubt she even knew what we watched on TV; she always seemed preoccupied, her glass of wine or scotch and water always by her side. There was usually little conversation between Mom and me. She was so very mournfully quiet, wearing a sad face most of the time.

My brother had decided college was not for him after a semester and enlisted in the Navy. He was away, except for occasional leaves, but he did call as often as he could.

I made a constant effort to make Mom happy through achievements, nothing unusual for any child. I enjoyed school, so this did not take extra energy on my part. My grades were excellent and Mom seemed to take the good grades for granted.

The mother I knew as a very young child was not to re-surface for almost twenty years. Youthful resilience, some luck, good friends and teachers paved my way towards adolescence.

MARIE WEBER   ROBERT GARRETT
Married the class president. .. ... the boy she married

MOM

The Keys to My Kingdom

P<small>ART OF MY PERFECT</small> 1950s family life was taking piano lessons. My mother played the piano, and her sisters were all musically inclined, as they humbly put it. It was considered part of a young lady's education and taken very seriously.

You could tell time by my piano practice schedule--each weekday at approximately four p.m. It did not normally take threats, persuasion or bribery to get me to practice. Being a normal child, however, I did balk occasionally, due to an overwhelming desire to watch *The Mickey Mouse Club* instead. But ultimately I played scales, scales and more scales to loosen the fingers and promote dexterity. Then on to the waltzes, sonatas and preludes. The only two days I did not practice were Sunday (day of rest) and Tuesday. Tuesday was the day of my weekly lesson. The matter was a simple one. I loved playing the piano and I adored my piano teacher, Leona Gerber.

I began piano lessons in 1953 at age six. My mother picked me up from school and drove me to my teacher's house. The house was nestled among tall pine trees on top of a hill overlooking a large lake, appropriately named Pines Lake. The large log house looked like something out of a fairy tale. Entering through the front porch and removing my shoes to keep her carpet clean, I stepped into a large living room, furnished with heavy wood frame couches and chairs with big, soft cushions. There were heavy drapes on the six-foot-high windows. The cathedral ceilings in that room were trimmed by huge log beams. Best of all was an impressive, black, shiny grand piano.

I was warmly greeted by Mrs.Gerber, a petite lady with a very sweet smile, beautiful skin and a smooth dark pageboy with bangs. I was ushered into her "modern" kitchen for an after-school snack before beginning my lesson. Each week it was the same: a piece of fruit, two cookies and Mrs. Gerber's unique drink, a blend of Pepsi and milk. I never had anything like it before or since. The "Gerber theory" was that I needed the vitamins in the milk because I was so skinny, but that I also deserved a touch of sugar after a long day at school. I got used to the taste, but it was never a beverage of choice. We would chat in her kitchen while I ate my snack. I remember her kind demeanor and soft voice. She would listen to my chatter about the school day or about music. I could not talk about classical music with my friends, lest I be labeled dull and boring. Mrs. Gerber was the grown-up in my life who would listen and comment but not judge or reprimand like a parent. She was interested in all of her students as young people, not only as music students. I was indeed very lucky to have this gracious lady in my life.

My lesson would then begin after a visit to the sink to wash my hands; Mrs. Gerber told me this was important, as clean hands showed respect for the instrument (and also kept cookie crumbs off her grand piano). I sat down at the magnificent instrument with happy anticipation. I was enthralled with every piece she taught me to play. I loved the melodies and different tempos but most of all, I loved the sound that piano made, so resonant and rich, filling the room with sounds of Chopin, Mozart, Tchaikovsky and a smattering of Hungarian Rhapsodies by Franz Liszt. I loved the touch of the ivory, as smooth as a baby's skin; each stroke of a key was a treat for the sense of touch. When Mrs. Gerber played for me to show me the way a piece should be played, I was in awe of how her small and delicate hands that could show such strength when the composer called for it.

Mrs. Gerber taught with a unique sensitivity to the needs of each student, most likely one of the reasons she was so well liked by her young protégés. She knew that my first love was dance. Therefore, while learning "Dance of the Hours," she would tell me, "Leanne, your fingers should almost dance on the keys like a ballerina doing tiny graceful jumps!" It made me feel that this piece was composed especially for me and that she had picked it out especially for me to play. This feeling motivated me to put more of myself into playing the piece.

All of Mrs. Gerber's students learned not only how to play the piano but were given an education in music not found in any elementary school. She believed that her students should know about the composers whose work they were learning to play. I read about each composer's life and career as I played his work so that I could have a better understanding of his music. I studied Beethoven, Chopin, Mozart, Grieg, Franz Liszt and other classical masters. Each time I finished the study of a composer, Mrs.Gerber presented me with a small, white marble statuette of the artist.

Occasionally, my mother and I went to Newark, NJ with Mrs.Gerber where at the time, the New Jersey Symphony Orchestra performed special concerts for young people. My favorite part was watching the conductor direct the orchestra, with his flowing, dramatic movements.

In June of each year, a recital was held at which each student performed one or two pieces. My mother and I shopped for a new, frilly pink dress to make the night complete. Mrs. Gerber had high standards; I tried to live up to that ideal and I think it must have been apparent in my performance. I always did well and felt exhilarated and excited after each performance. When I heard the applause and saw the smiling faces in the audience, a wonderful feeling of warmth came over me; people I didn't even know liked the music I had shared; I had given them some of the happiness I felt when playing. I still remember the proud faces of my mother and father at the performances, as well as the annoyed look on my brother's face for having to be there at all.

Because of my father's untimely death, he was not at my final piano recital; my best performance at my most advanced level. My mother, brother and I had to move out of the area and adjust to a much different lifestyle, putting an end to my piano lessons at age eleven. Our piano was sold because there was no room for it in our new home. My music lessons were temporarily lost as part of the trauma of our family tragedy.

I often say a little thank you to Leona Gerber when I hear a favorite concerto, symphony or rhapsody. She taught me that music is not merely notes written on a page but the passion, depth and life's breath of the composer. Since childhood, I have expanded my love of music from the classics to include musical theater, spiritual hymns, Dixieland, folk music, swing, some opera, bluegrass and a splash of pop/rock and doo wop.

I cannot imagine my world without music. Thank you, Mrs. Gerber.

Rites
of
Passage

Fitting In

MOVING FROM OUR LARGE HOUSE into a two-bedroom top floor apartment was probably the biggest cultural shock I could have ever had in my eleven-year old state at that time. What, no pantry off the kitchen? No room of my own? No spacious yard or field filled with wild flowers? No deer coming to pick the fruit off the apple trees?

Even our dog, John Spotswood, a.k.a, Spotty, was disoriented for a few days. We now had to put him on a leash and walk him instead of letting him out the back door and hooking him up to a rope on a cable where he had the run of one of the yards. A few days after we moved in to the apartment, there was a knock at the door. It was our landlord.

"You know, you did not tell me you have a dog and I do not want your dog here." I could see the tears form in Mom's eyes and my stomach started churning. Mom was left with no choice. She started looking for someone to take our thirteen-year-old loyal family friend. About a week later, around seven p.m. Mom answered our doorbell. I was surprised that she seemed to know the man. He had brought a leash and began to hook up John Spotswood, (who was being his friendly tail-wagging self) petting him while smiling and saying, "What a good dog you are, and you're so handsome!" Spotty was always responsive to a few friendly words and a scratch behind the ears. I was starting to get upset, realizing what was about to happen. Mom then explained that this was the town pet control man. He had found a farm in New York State that was going to take Spotty. He would have lots of room to run and the people who lived on the farm would treat him very well.

"You can't give our Spotty away," I cried, tears streaming down my face. While the man led our dog down the stairs, Mom held me tightly, trying to comfort me and also to restrain me so I would not run after them. Spotty was still happily wagging his tail, thinking this new friend was taking him for a walk. Mom and I were both crying by then. I went into the bedroom and cried for the remainder of the night. My memory of that night is vivid. When John Spotswood walked out the door, in my child's mind, I felt that another precious living thing in my world was gone forever. The hardest part this time was that Spotty, being a dog, did not understand. I figured that he must be confused and upset because I didn't have the time to explain things to him about his new family and the farm. I spent another few days in tearful emotional turmoil and vowed never to own another pet.

I started the seventh grade in the fall of 1959. My interests still remained with music and dancing. Desperate to fit in with my new classmates and belong to this new environment, I tried to get into the popular tunes of the times. My idea of good music at that time was Beethoven's Fifth, not "In the Still of the Night." I listened to the popular tunes of that time over and over trying to learn most of the words so it would seem to the other kids that I knew them well. I was invited to some seventh grade parties where my new friends played spin the bottle. This was so foreign to me, I was still thinking about it for a few days after the party, trying to understand the reason why anyone would want to kiss whoever the spin landed on. I was too embarrassed to ask the other girls what it was all about; they seemed to think it was fun. At least they acted as if they did. Guess I was a late bloomer. Or maybe my hormones weren't raging enough.

I plodded on through seventh and eighth grades like most preteens, wondering what high school would be like, hoping I didn't get pimples and wondering if I would ever develop breasts. Then when I did, I discovered how uncomfortable bras were. I performed well academically and even ended up enjoying some of the social activities. The church youth group I had joined when first moving into town was still very important to me. I even asked the youth minister to give me a head start course in Algebra I because I was so anxious about having a hard time with the subject, knowing math was not my strong subject. What a patient man he was.

I was excited to enter high school in the fall of 1961. I

earned good grades, made the varsity cheerleading squad as a freshman and was active in student council. This put me just on the edge of the "cool" crowd, because I never "hung out" or went to parties or dated, I never felt that I really fit in.

I had finally started to dance again and did not have the time to "hang out." Dance classes had been another loss after Dad's death, but Mom realized how lost I was without dancing in my life and somehow managed to pay for classes As a result, I was usually too busy with classes and rehearsals at a local ballet school to have a full- time teen social life. I was so happy dancing, I didn't think much about it. One year, I was finally eligible to audition for the *corps de ballet* of a local well-known ballet company where I took my classes. They were going to perform the famous Tschaikovsky ballet, *Swan Lake* and this was my chance to audition for the company. I was selected at the audition to become a member of the company. I was beside myself with excitement and a feeling of real accomplishment. Ballet was not my forte; I was a much better musical theater performer but because I truly loved ballet, I was determined to improve at it. I practically exploded into our apartment after the audition. Mom was in the bedroom as usual.

"Mom, Mom, I made it! I made it!."

" Made what?," she said quietly. The look on her face made me stop in my tracks. She *knew* where I had been. I could not imagine how my own mother could not relate to the thrill of acceptance on her daughter's face. Again,

I made excuses for her, thinking maybe it had slipped her mind.

"Remember, I auditioned today for the company? Well, I was accepted. I am going to be in the corps for Swan Lake. I will be a Swan and maybe get to be one of the four Little Swans. Wouldn't that be fantastic? Isn't this just the best thing that's ever happened to me?"

"Oh that's nice, good for you." She answered, as though I had told her I had just brushed my teeth. No emotion, no warmth. I was crushed. I wanted desperately for her to be happy and proud (a hug would have been a bonus).

During two glorious summer vacations, I was selected by the ballet school I attended to go to Cape Cod for six weeks to study and perform—a unique experience I will always cherish. The small, reputable ballet company of the school was owned by a magnificent Russian lady from a famous Russian family of choreographers, the Fokines. Miss Fokine rented an old house in Cape Cod, which was once two small lighthouses. The former owner had made the two lighthouses into bedrooms, with spiral staircases from the first to the second floors in each lighthouse. There was a living room with a huge fireplace built in between the two lighthouse/bedrooms with a kitchen and bathroom added onto the original kitchen in the back of the house. Another small guest house was built on the property with a very large deck, which we used as our dancing studio. We had classes outside on the deck for three hours in the morning and again in the late afternoon. In the early afternoon, we went to the beach, relaxed or took our turns at household chores. There was no complaining as we had so much fun doing even cleaning and cooking for fifteen people. At night, we put on little skits, which our beautiful Russian ballet mistress would take part in. At the end of the summer, we received mock medals for our performances made out of the tops of canned goods, with ribbon glued around the edges. For two consecutive years, I was the "Greatest Little Comedian." Here, in this sheltered dance world, I fit in.

Summer at CAPE COD, dancing

During my second summer there, I got a call from our high school class advisor back home. "Hey, Leanne, after your audition last May, we decided that you should play Kim McAfee, one of the female leads in our fall production of *Bye Bye Birdie*. The other dancers in the living room at the time I got the call could not fathom at first why I was jumping and leaping, while shouting, "I got it! I got it!" My world became perfect that day at sixteen years old. Ballet and the lead in a musical comedy—it couldn't get any better than that for me.

Back in school that fall, the play went very well. "*Bye*

Bye Birdie" is the perfect play for a high school audience and we really had fun performing the '50s rock 'n roll music with an Elvis -like character as the male lead and my swooning teenage fan role.

After the play was over, I decided I wanted to earn some money of my own. I was tired of asking Mom for everything; maybe I could even start saving for a car. I thought a job in a store would be a good idea. We lived close to a small city with bus service that stopped right outside our apartment building. I thought through all the practicalities that I knew Mom would throw at me when I approached her with this idea; I had done my research and was ready with all the right answers. I would have to sacrifice cheerleading for the season, but it would be worth it. After all, I was maturing. I needed to move on.

Mom came in from work and I was ready. After dinner, she poured some wine and started into the bedroom, her usual retreat for the evening. "Mom, I would like to apply for a part-time job at Meyer Brothers. A few of my friends work there and it's not too many hours a week and the bus stops right outside the door so I wouldn't be walking in Paterson at all ever, so it's really safe. I could work Saturdays too, so that would be good and I would reeeally like to earn some money of my own, pleeease?"

"No," she said. "I don't want you riding on a bus to or from Paterson at night."

"Well, what if I found someone I knew with the same schedule to ride with, would that be okay?" I had thought of all her objections and was ready with the comebacks. She was silent for a moment. She took a sip of wine.

"I guess you could try it, as long as your grades stay as good as they are," she relented.

"Oh, thank you, thank you, thank you." I went to call my girlfriend to tell her I could go fill out an application the next day with her. I joined the ranks of part-time after school workers. I felt like I fit in.

Wearing the required uniform, I boarded the bus for the first bus ride of my life to my first job. I felt so professional, so grown up. On my first day, I was assigned to the lingerie department. The store was generally frequented by mature women and had a quiet conservative atmosphere. We were required to wear a navy blue skirt, white blouse and a navy blue cardigan (I felt like I was in Catholic school). This being my first job, I learned an abundance of things about the nature of women shoppers and women in general. I learned that many who are large of stature don't realize that they are of large stature and will try to fit into lingerie that is too small. I learned that men and women were not meant to shop for underwear together because men, even if they have been married to the women for many years, are embarrassed by this type of shopping. I learned that when it comes to a sale, there is nothing, *nothing* a woman will not do to latch onto a bargain, especially if it is the last in their size. I witnessed women who walked into my department, some pleasant, some tight-lipped and serious. These were well-spoken women who turned into screaming witches, pulling items from one another, pushing each other aside and cutting into lines. I thought at first the lingerie department would be boring; it was anything but. I learned to fold, fold, fold a lot of panties which is maybe why now, my bureau drawers are so messy all of the time.

That job lasted for about eight months until I decided I really wasn't ready to be all that mature yet and went back to cheerleading the following year, my senior year. I did, however, have fun with the money I earned and no, I saved nothing for a car.

During my last summer of high school, I went on a six-week tour of Europe for six weeks with other students and several teachers as chaperones. It was there I learned what the teenage meaning of "partying" was. Most of the kids had already started drinking at parties on the weekends. The state north of where I lived had a lower drinking age. Some of the group would go on Saturdays and drink with fake ID they would beg or borrow (or steal) from an older sibling, cousin or friend. They went on those jaunts; I danced. But in Europe, alcohol was readily available if you were tall enough to see over the bar. I quickly became acquainted with it and poof! I felt a part of things instantly. I had a newfound confidence in my own personality, a curiously comfortable self-esteem never realized before. A new person emerged and I really liked her. And WHAM, I felt like I fit in like never before!

My senior year was a lot better socially. I met my first love and despite my still active dancing life, I did manage to have a more normal teenage life. He did not live in the town I lived in, so we did not spend a lot of time with my friends, but mostly with his friends from his school. This was fine with me, because I was with *him*, the one, the only. He was a lot of fun to be with, smart and knew so much about everything. He was athletic. He wrote poetry. He paid attention to me. He thought I was cute and funny. Having a boyfriend gave me self confidence, a new type of self-esteem different from the kind that performing gave me; this was the real me that he liked, not the person on the stage whose talent got the applause. We went to the prom, to the beach—all the things normal teens do. I felt connected. I fit in.

As I entered my senior year in high school, Mom retreated to the bedroom nightly after dinner, no TV, coming out only to refill her drink. Many years later, I realized this was really the progression of her depression and alcoholism. Both took their effect on a beautiful lady who got lost after a tragic life's turn which changed her happy life.

As for me, I consciously felt very little effect now from mom's behavior. I rarely thought I was deprived of any parental guidance or support; I just didn't think about that aspect of my life: I built a shield around me and went about my days living in my own teen world. I thought my best friend's mother, who was younger than my mom, was the most wonderful mother there was. My friend and I would talk with her about all the important "stuff" that girls wanted to know that I would never think to talk about with my mom. The other stable factor in my life was my church and their youth group which I had joined when we first moved into town. This became my refuge those first few years, starting at the age of twelve. The youth ministers were my anchor. The friends I made there had stable families and opened their homes to me. My brother who joined the Navy after trying college called often to make sure Mom and I were doing okay and my aunt stayed close by too. Although these people were fixtures in my life, I felt no deep emotional tie to them or anyone except of course my girlfriend.

High school graduation was coming soon. Probably the most courageous decision my mother made as a parent was to realize that I needed to be away from her and go away to college. This meant she would be completely without the last connection she had to my dad.

When I went to college, I basked in all of the freedom that most freshman feel being away from parental control for a prolonged period of time. I was responsible for me. Classes went well since I was always an eager student. I was so excited about the theater program and loved the difference in the college atmosphere compared to high school—everyone there wanted to be there.

Weekends were awesome. I was introduced to a whole new substance—beer. I did not drink in high school except for my one European experience. I was busy with dance rehearsals and did not do the whole teen party drinking scene with many of my classmates—another reason why I never quite fit in, always felt socially just on the edge of the popular crowd even though I did have a really close girl friend who didn't care if I spent a lot of time elsewhere. Now in college, it was different. I went to parties every weekend where the alcohol was flowing and it actually tasted pretty good. After having a few drinks, a feeling of such social well being came over me that I really enjoyed myself; dancing, making friends. . .fitting in. It was in college that I really fit in with the help of this really close weekend friend. . . alcohol.

Dance

THE JOY THAT DANCING BRINGS to me is almost indescribable. When I move to beautiful music, my mental and physical makeup blissfully become one; my body is my own. It is the most exquisite ecstasy I have ever felt. As a very young child I felt such exhilaration and happiness when dancing that I developed a devotion towards having that feeling again and again and so I continued studying throughout my childhood and adolescence. When I dance, I know what to do with my body to evoke emotion I find impossible to express in any other way. It can be laughter, tears, flirtation, fun or excitement; my body is my own to express those things.

A powerful, intoxicating rhythm pulsates in my body like a heartbeat. When I hear the music and begin to dance, I move to the rhythm, making it my own. If the beat goes faster, faster, faster, it stirs up more dramatic swaying, turning, turning, turning off the outside world for just a few moments in time, letting only the excitement of the dance shine through.

At the climax of the music, as if ignited by a spark of fire, I triumphantly leap through the air lifting my heart to the peak of intoxication. My head held high, my face radiant and smiling, expressing my hope that this joy reaches those who watch so they share in the experience of happiness deep within me.

Dance will forever remain the passionate expression of my soul.

My 15 Minutes of Fame!

MY COLLEGE CURRICULUM CONSISTED OF required courses for graduation with a degree in a major of secretarial science. I filled the rest of my schedule with theater classes. The college I decided on and obtained acceptance to offered an excellent theater program and my sights (as well as my heart) were set on a career in the musical theater. In two years, I would have an associate degree in business, giving me "something to fall back on," as my mother reminded me so many times.

The newly built state-of-the-art theater, Theatre '59 opened that year with a production of *Carousel*. Gordon MacRae revived his leading role of stage and screen as Billy Bigelow. A very young, talented Texan, named Tommy Tune, took on one of his first jobs after coming to New York City as our choreographer. He was very professional; it was a wonderful experience for a young dancer like me to work with him. I thought heaven must be like this.

That summer of 1966 brought acceptance as an apprentice at a summer stock theater company in Long Island, N.Y. As an apprentice, I would be joining a group of young hopefuls who would build sets, sew costumes, paint, act as ushers and (hopefully) perform. I saved every penny from part- time jobs to spend six weeks there (not only did apprentices receive no salary, we had to pay for room and board). Experience would be our pay. Some of the apprentices were college students like me. Others my age had been trying for their big break in NewYork for a few years. I envied the total commitment they gave to their dream and the courage it took to rebel against parental pressure to find a "real job." Back then, I saw only the excitement of their lives, not the heartache, rejection and ever-present poverty and insecurity.

The playhouse was on the grounds of an old estate. There was a theater, a large home converted into dormitory-style living quarters, an old barn turned into classrooms, dance studios and a studio/costume shop. After the last curtain call each night, we'd spend hours relaxing around an old, broken concrete swimming pool built in the 1930s with columns and cracked Greek statues. There we spent the only down time of our day, drinking, smoking, talking, improvising and dreaming about our futures in musical theater.

There were two distinct levels of summer residents in summer stock theater. At the top were the professional performers who were contracted by the Board of Directors for the season to play the leading roles in the musicals. Some were "rising young stars" hired to play leading men and female ingénue roles such as Nelly in *South Pacific* or Daisy Mae in *L'il Abner*. Ken Howard played the part of L'il Abner that year and the young lieutenant in *South Pacific*. He went on to be a very successful actor in films and television. The apprentices were the lower level of this mini society. However, we were in no way discouraged by this unwritten fact of life in the show biz world. In 1966 we were nineteen or twenty years old, talented and optimistic about where our talent would take us.

Our typical day started with classes in dance, voice and drama. We built sets or made costumes in the early afternoon and rehearsed for the next production until about five p.m. Then we prepared for that evening's performance of the show that was currently running. During that summer, I performed in the popular musicals of my generation: *Li'l Abner, South Pacific* and *Oliver*. Weekends were for Children's Matinees. Playing Dopey in *Snow White and the Seven Dwarfs* was one of my "most fun I ever had" moments. What could compare with making children and adults laugh by singing "ho hum the music's dumb / the words don't mean a thing/ Isn't this a silly song for anyone to sing?" in an oversized mask with giant caricature features of Dopey the Dwarf and dancing with six other young dancers dressed as the other dwarfs? It was quite a contrast to the role of a prostitute I played in *Oliver*.

As a group, we got along well. This was very important since we had to work, play, study, eat, sleep and perform together twenty-four hours a day, seven days a week. Inevitably, a few summer romances developed. I remember having a crush on one of the other dancers. He seemed to like me, too. We spent hours talking in the evenings, so I couldn't understand why there was no progress in the romance department. One day, another one of the male dancers took pity on my naiveté. He took me aside and said in his kindest voice, "Sweetheart, don't you notice that Frank hangs around exclusively with me, Tom, Mark and José? You know, we socialize and 'be' with each other."

"Sure he does. You are all friends and you dance together," I replied. " I still don't get why he takes no interest in me romantically. We really like each other."

"Of course he does. You're a terrific girl, but he'll never be interested in you THAT way. He's GAY."

"You mean he only likes guys?" I was uncharacteristically speechless after saying that, my eyes welling up with tears, understandably shocked. This was 1966. Alternative lifestyles were still at the "closet" stage, so this was my very first gay experience. I was very embarrassed, more for my lack of street smarts than Frank's sexual preference. After I understood Frank's lifestyle, he and I remained friends in a much more relaxed way.

When I returned to college in September 1966 for the fall semester, I continued working in musical theater. Performances included *Stop the World, I Want to Get Off,* a few variety revues with Tommy Tune returning as choreographer and an annual competition of original musical comedy spoofs for Homecoming Week. Our team's *November Nonsense* won first place for our patriotic theme against draft dodging. It was then that I got a taste of writing, directing and choreography. *Another* 5 minutes of fame.

By the way, Mom was right--I have used that degree I earned to "fall back on"--- thanks, Mom. It turned out, I was not to be Broadway bound after all. Fate brought my life journey in another direction and the family life I chose has brought me the best years of my life. However, in Leanne's "Book of Life" the 1965-67 chapter will remain a favorite.

At First Sight

Amazing crystal blue eyes as brilliant as the blue of a
     cloudless summer sky, coupled with an intoxicating
smile that lights up the space that surrounds him.
     He melted my heart in that one instant so many years ago.

A special charm, warmth and wit,
     A true portrait of his rich Irish heritage
Honest, forthright, a gentleman.......
     Strong and independent, a private man.

He was brought up with love, high value and morality,
     He served his country well, a hero.
He came home to ungrateful peers,
     building his future, renewing a good life.

This man so attracted my love and…
     Hallelujah! that love was returned to me!
We became one, united to prosper and grow, together.
     To weather life's storms and rainbows ever after.

His quiet intellect, logical mind and integrity
     carries him through a stellar career
Success after success nationwide fulfills his earnest desire
     to succeed; to provide the best for those he loves.

Not perfect, he longs to fix it all; he works too long and too hard,
    seen by all who benefit from his talent and leadership.
His intensity admirable, we urge him to take more time
    to enjoy those fruits he has labored for.

If only this era could see more men like him.
    A presence respected, this cherished love of mine.
His family gives most meaning to him; he is so proud.
    His quiet love, always giving; his delight in our little ones.

He and I are now partners, best friends, one.
    A love that comes with the true test of time.
At first sight, I somehow knew I could love him
    with a passion, faithfulness and goodness he so richly
    deserves.

Marriage
and Children
and Life,
OH MY!

The Bride's Nightmare

THE MOST IMPORTANT DAY OF my life had arrived. I was getting married to the most wonderful guy in the world. I was dressing for my big day; the bridal party was gathered at my home, laughing, primping; a happy excited atmosphere prevailed. Then the phone rang.

"It's the florist," my mother yelled from downstairs.

"The shipment of white tea roses never arrived. Is there something else you'd like for your bouquet?" Oh no, strike one.

While I was putting on my makeup, enjoying the anticipation of the beautiful ceremony Bob and I had planned, the phone rang again, making my stomach do a flip-flop. Mom came into my room looking totally distressed, tears welling up in her beautiful brown eyes.

"That was Uncle Bill," she began. "Aunt Harriet had a heart attack and is in the hospital. The doctor says he thinks she will recover. Of course, your aunt, uncle, Sue and Bill Jr. won't be coming to the wedding." Strike two.

While putting my beautiful wedding gown on over my head, I tried to remain calm. Surely nothing more could happen to put a damper on this special day. Suddenly the sky began to darken to a shade of dark, purple-gray. I heard thunder rumbling and out of the corner of my eye, saw drops of rain appear on the walk to the patio near the back door. Then suddenly, a bolt of lightning struck a tree in our back yard. Hailstones as big as quarters then began to plummet from the heavens.

My brother shouted, "Oh my God, there goes the reception tent!" I shut my eyes and put head between my knees to keep from fainting. Panic set in....*three strikes and we're out!*

Instead of fainting, I awoke with a slight headache. The dream was one of the worst nightmares I have ever had.

I showered and dressed for work quickly that morning. I was going to my job at an educational book publishing company early that day so I could take an extended lunch hour. Bob and I were going to the Borough Clerk's office to apply for our marriage license. The morning at work crept along; I could not concentrate on my work. The vivid dream about my wedding day clouded my thoughts. No one's wedding day could be *that* disastrous, could it? In reality we were not planning a large wedding like the one in my dream, but even at a small ceremony I guessed things could go wrong. Bob arrived at 11:45 a.m. to begin the short drive to the municipal offices in our town. Without warning, a very large, entirely black cat ran across the road in front of our car. Bob slammed on the brakes, just missing the furry beast. After a seemingly interminable silence within the car, we looked at each other and giggled nervously.

"I don't believe in that silly superstition about black cats crossing your path bringing bad luck, do you?" I asked Bob. "Of course not," he agreed, trying to ease my nervousness. We silently finished the trip to the municipal building, both trying to convince ourselves that this was just a silly little thing we would tell our grandchildren thirty years from now. We parked the car and entered the office building, still trying to laugh off the black cat incident. Upon exiting the elevator onto the second floor, we looked up and saw a sign on the Borough Clerk's office door:

CLOSED FOR LUNCH

We did not get a marriage license that day.

EPILOGUE: We did eventually get our license and have been together for many years. When our daughter called one day to ask if she could bring home a kitten, I asked one question, "Is it black?"

The Palace

ONE, TWO, THREE, FOUR . . .I started mentally counting the steps on my way up to look at the apartment for rent on the third floor of the old house. I wanted a concrete idea of exactly how many steps I would be dealing with on a daily basis if this place was "the one." I started losing my breath around the second floor. I was four months pregnant. My husband was currently serving his last few months in the army, stationed at a base in the south. I was living with my mom in the northern New Jersey, still working at my secretarial job to save money for our own place when he was discharged.

There were forty-one steps. The landlord turned around, took one look at me and asked with a concerned look on his little round face, "Are you okay, sweetheart?" Since I had not mentioned a soon to be third, smaller tenant, I looked at him, smiled brightly and said, "Oh sure, just not used to all those steps. Let's take a look at the apartment, shall we?" He unlocked the door and we walked through a small entryway into a freshly painted, bright, large, open room. It was a good thing it was large, because it was to be our living room, kitchen and dining room. Along one wall was a countertop with a sink, two stove top burners and a tiny refrigerator. There were kitchen cabinets above and below the sink area. That was the kitchen. I noted one thing missing: an oven. Maybe that toaster oven we got for a wedding gift would now come in handy.

The next room I saw was the bathroom, about 14' by 15' in size. My first thought was that we could have a small party in there, putting lots of ice and drinks in the old fashioned claw-foot white porcelain tub. There was also a shower head on a pole installed for the die-hard shower-taker. My second thought was, "How will I ever climb into this tub when I am nine months pregnant?"

The last room across the small foyer was an enormous dormered room (this apartment was previously an attic). If you stood at one end, you felt like you had been swallowed by Jonah's whale in the Old Testament story from the Bible. This was to be our bedroom and den/family room/library/music room and maybe nursery all rolled into one. There was also a tiny separate room off the bedroom to be used as the one and only closet (you needed to put up a freestanding rack to hang up your clothes).This had a window with a fire escape attached. It was good to know the landlord followed safety codes. In case of fire, if you could get past every possession you owned that was shoved inside this small space, you might be saved from a fiery death -- that is, if you could open the window that looked like it had been painted shut.

In the last two days, I had looked at so many places that were dirty, overpriced and in questionable areas. I was exhausted, discouraged and missing my husband in so many ways. This place seemed like heaven to me. It was very clean, newly painted and CHEAP. "I'll take it," I said, trying to restrain my urge to hug this short pudgy man. He seemed a bit surprised, but we sealed the deal with a signature and a deposit. After that, I was on my way to make a phone call with very good news to tell.

We moved in with two old chairs from my in-laws' finished basement, a few folding TV tray tables, and a folding card table for our dining area table. That was the extent of our furniture for the moment Along with some helpful friends, we huffed and puffed with boxes and clothes up the three long flights of stairs. Oh yes, we did have a dresser for the bedroom and the bed was coming from the department store. We were smiling from ear to ear . . .we were *home.*

When the delivery truck arrived with our bed, the men asked where the bed, box spring and mattress were going. When we pointed up, their reaction was less than happy. When we got to the steps, which were rather narrow, they became a bit concerned. When they walked up the three flights to the door of the apartment, they shook their heads and said to my husband, "There ain't no way any full size bed gonna fit through here, mister."

My eyes started to well up. I did not want to cry, but

this was going to ruin our big day in a big way. I wanted everything to go perfectly. I was even planning a lovely first dinner, cooked in our brand new, just-out-of-the-box toaster oven. The delivery men just wanted to leave and let us deal with the store service representatives. My husband, however, is a problem solver. He convinced them that by taking off the frosted piece of Plexiglas next to the doorway, they could hand the mattress and box spring through to the large hallway that led into the bedroom. We got our bed. We had our first night in our new home. While lying on our backs in our new bed at one end of a long, cavernous bedroom, we felt very small, very tired and very happy to be starting our new life in our own private palace.

Confessions of a
Non-Compliant Convert

I DIDN'T FALL IN LOVE, I catapulted, head first. My prince charming was a handsome Irish Catholic young man. I fell in love with his warmth, wit, sense of humor, honesty and oh, those magnificent crystal clear blue eyes! He had a brief time left in the Army. We had no patience for long engagements, so a few months before discharge, we married in a small church of my Protestant denomination. It was the late '60s; we were very much in love, excited, a bit frightened and we didn't have a dime to our name.

My husband was raised in a close, loving family. He had an older sister and one younger brother. I soon came to love his family with their secure, "normal" life, My new family seemed more complete, since for me, there had been only Mom and me since I was eleven. My brother had been away from home most of the time since his eighteenth birthday; first at college, then serving in the Navy, then married. My new husband's family immediately embraced me as a member of their family, which I accepted with a feeling of completeness I had not known before.

We soon began our family with the coming birth of our first baby. I seriously considered converting to Catholicism. Although I was a WASP (White Anglo Saxon Protestant) through and through, I reasoned that Protestants and Catholics both held similar beliefs about Christ and Christian love. However, the laws and rituals of each denomination were very different. I read more about Roman Catholicism and felt I would not be giving up any beliefs that I already had; I would only be adding some new observances, rituals and celebratory services. The adjustments I would need to make had to do with mere manmade laws. The major changes would be the Roman Catholic belief in the Pope and the sacrament of Penance. I was confident that education would help me with these.

My mother-in-law voiced her concern without hesitation. "Lee, don't do it." (She was not one to mince words). She wanted me to be sure I was not doing this only to please my husband (and her). I assured her this was not the case. Bob and I talked about this step many times at great length. It had been left completely up to me. I explained how eager I was for family unity in something as important as this. I was vaguely confused by my mother-in-law's misgivings; I had anticipated that she would have been extremely happy about this step.

I began going to mass weekly. The differences in the service seemed quite mysterious at first. My initial thought was, "Where are those hearty voices of the congregation raised in song with praise for the Lord?" That's what I was used to in my church. I learned that for the most part, Catholic congregations (back then, in the '60s) did not sing loudly, if at all. Some I spoke with told me the Church had tried repeatedly over the years to promote better participation with worship through more contemporary hymns and spiritual music. They were evidently still trying.

The time came for my instruction to begin. Father John was a kind man. He explained the course of instruction and then asked me the name of the parish where Bob and I had been married. Upon learning that our marriage had taken place in a Christian Reformed church by a Christian Reformed minister, the priest's face lost color as he tried, unsuccessfully, to control his distress.

"Since your husband is a Catholic and was not married in the Catholic Church, he has been living in sin for the entire time of your marriage and his soul is in grave danger!" he said. He did not seem in the least bit concerned for *my* soul, as if *my* soul meant something less because I was Protestant. This line of thinking did not seem very Christian-like, but I continued to listen as the priest told me that Bob and I must be married again as soon as possible in the rectory (we were not to taint the sanctity of the main cathedral with our disgrace), before the Catechism instruction could continue. And so we went through a second marriage ceremony--but, this time it was HOLY matrimony. The white dress I borrowed was several sizes larger because of my pregnancy. What a sight to behold--- an eight-month pregnant woman and her errant sinner of a husband! Our families decided that this would be a wedding long remembered. After all, most couples only have one anniversary.

Next was to be my first confession. Growing up, I had been active in my church. As part of our prayers, we were taught to pray to God and Jesus, asking for forgiveness for our transgressions, strength and guidance in our lives. I now would be speaking through a mediator of sorts in the business of forgiveness negotiation (my terminology). I was properly schooled on the formalities of the sacrament. As I sat in the church waiting my turn, I watched other confessors. Did they look relieved upon leaving the confessional, being verbally absolved of all of their sins? Were they peaceful and guilt-free after doing their assigned penance? One young woman exited the confessional already praying softly. A young man came out with a look on his face that was anything but peaceful; I wondered what his sin must have been. A small boy, about eleven years of age, ran out crying to his mother. That one was difficult for me to judge. I waited, hopeful that my experience would be a more joyful, one with a feeling of immediate exoneration.

When my turn came to enter the confessional, I felt nervous, almost as if I was going to meet God Himself on Judgement Day. I entered the small, cramped confessional and the screen opened. "Bless me, Father, for I have sinned," I uttered softly, "This is my first confession." The priest said, "Speak up, I can't hear a word you're saying, dear." I proceeded with the list of sins I had committed in a slightly louder voice, hoping no one outside the confessional would hear me. I was becoming a bit claustrophobic by now, so I tried to focus more on the task at hand. The process seemed to go quickly then; after all, I hadn't committed any of the "biggies": murder, theft or adultery. Realizing I was an adult "first-timer, " the priest than chatted about confession in general. He instructed me to say some prayers for penance, absolved me of my sins with a prayer. As I walked to the church pew to sit and pray, my first thought was relief that I was over that nervous first-time feeling you get when something is new and out of your comfort zone. I then sat down and prayed, which always made me feel peaceful and close to God. However, I did not feel that I really needed to talk to a priest to have him intercede or tell me how to be forgiven. I went to read a bit more about this sacrament.. I ultimately made a difficult decision which went against the manmade law in Catholicism; to continue talking to God on my own. It had worked for me. So much for the sacrament of Penance.

Years passed without another formal confession to Father Tim (or any other Father). I did pass all the other requirements to become a Catholic and was eventually confirmed. Our first daughter had been baptized in the Church and is still a happy Catholic.

About 3 years later, another adorable daughter joined our family. It was soon time for both girls to begin their religious education. Both girls disliked their CCD (Confraternity of Christian Doctrine) classes from the start; it became a real chore for me to get them to go to classes. I had difficulty understanding why. I had always loved Sunday School as a child. Then, I realized that the girls were not learning much and there was little instruction about the Bible. Instead, there were a lot of rules, Catechism and oh yes, guilt.

During summer vacation, a neighborhood Baptist Church held a Vacation Bible School for one week. Being an ecumenical kind of gal, I enrolled both girls. They loved each and every day they went to class. My daughters learned the hymns easily and were happy learning Bible verses. Games and songs were used as learning tools. All of the children came out of the church each day smiling, some singing songs they had learned. I knew the two basic doctrines were not so different, so it must be the methods of teaching that caused the children to react so adversely to one and enjoy the other.

I voiced my frustration and concern about the direction of my children's religious education to my mother-in-law. She just smiled her lovely Irish smile and said, "I seem to recall having a conversation a long time ago and in that conversation, I told you I thought you might someday decide that converting was not the best idea. Family happiness does not always rely on practicing the same organized religion."

I will always remember my mother-in-law's cheerful tolerance to my initial zealous approach to Catholicism. I valued her insight into family life. Here was a woman,

I had come to understand, who loved her church. But, having sent her children to Catholic school and centering much of her family's life around the church, she also realized its shortcomings as an organizational entity and managed to keep things in proper perspective.

Our daughters continued their Catholic education and I calmed down. I decided the disruption of changing them would be very confusing and their education was certainly guiding them in the right direction. In the end, I believe it is the examples they got at home that sealed the deal for their future.

I have since made peace with my conscience. I long ago confessed to God that I was sorry I did not go to see Father Tim again after that first experience in the confessional. I am sure he did not miss me, as no doubt he had enough compliant Catholic sinners to worry about.

God Bless, Praise the Lord, Hallelujah and Amen.

None other than Motherhood

Bᴏʙ ᴡʜᴇᴇʟᴇᴅ ᴍᴇ ɪɴᴛᴏ ᴛʜᴇ hospital after a frantic, just-like-a-scene-in-the-movies drive from our apartment around 7:00 p.m. on Sunday, March 16, the night before St. Patrick's Day. My labor had progressed very quickly for a first child. We had to hurry, as we were a good half-hour from the hospital, very nervous and clueless about labor and childbirth (no Lamaze classes back then). Bob was not too familiar with the location of the hospital, but I had told him, "Don't worry honey, when it's time to go, I can tell you how to get there. The hospital is not far off the exit from the highway." The meaning of "time to go" turned out to have a more urgent meaning than anticipated. The pain was a bit more intense than I expected, so I found I was in no shape to give coherent directions. Bob normally wouldn't have minded that I was squeezing his hand very hard, but it did make it difficult for him to shift gears at the same time. My head came up off the seat where my pain-ridden, distorted body lay to see where we were and to tell him or point where to turn. I confess to taking the Lord's name in vain each time a contraction came, which now was about every two minutes. I would shout, "Oh, Jesus, Mary and Joseph---GO LEFT!"

We did get to the hospital in one piece and Dr. O'Reilly greeted us at the door with "Couldn't ya have waited 'til midnight now, Mrs. Flanagan, far this Irish babe ta come inta th' world?" He laughed out loud when he saw the look I gave him, since he did not really have an Irish brogue and was trying to be amusing. He noticed I was not in the mood to be amused. Actually one of my thoughts at that time was, "How could any woman in her right mind voluntarily go through this more than once in her life?" Well, our beautiful Colleen could not wait. I guess it was more important to her to be a "Sunday's Child" than be born on St. Patrick's Day, so she entered our world about 9:00 p.m. Dr. O'Reilly was not to get his wish. He was also disappointed that I had interrupted the TV show he was watching in the doctor's lounge with a popular singer of the day, Jack Cassidy, singing Irish songs.

I was twenty-one years old. Never held an infant or toddler. Never leaned over a bassinet and said, "coo, coo, coo, baby, aren't you cute." Never babysat as a teenager. Never changed a diaper.

I had just given birth to a beautiful baby girl. There was not one intelligent idea in my head as to how I was going to handle this and somehow, I was not worried---yet. I was in a hospital and they would take care of it, right? Of course, Bob would be visiting every day too. Well, that would not be the case either. It turned out he had been fighting a cold and sore throat for a few days. After I gave birth, he went home to bed, exhausted and sick. He awoke about three a.m. with a high fever. One phone call to mom and dad and he was on his way to their house to stay with them. The next day, the doctor diagnosed tonsillitis. Bob was instructed to stay away from the hospital, the baby and me. For the next five days, I self-consciously told everyone who walked into my room that my husband was ill and could not visit. I felt insecure about the fact that I had no husband visiting like the other women and worried everyone would think I was an unwed mother (in 1969, that was a definite societal no-no).

I was determined to do all the "right" motherly things from the very beginning, so I began to nurse our baby. Things went well at the hospital and I could not wait until my little girl was brought to me every few hours. I went to a baby care class and got a little more confident in my ability to care for my beautiful little girl. My in-laws, who were thrilled with their first granddaughter (they already had a grandson), would bring me sweets, fruit and news of the other patient recuperating at their house. The doctor kept me in the hospital one extra day because Bob was ill. In those days, insurance was much more liberal. They actually paid benefits on the basis of the patient's condition and circumstance, not criteria in a book of regulations and codes about each diagnosis or condition.

My mother visited her new granddaughter after I called her and asked her to come; it was only a ten-minute ride from her apartment to the hospital. She was having problems with depression at that time and it was difficult for her to make an effort to go anywhere other than work. I thought seeing this wondrous new granddaughter, the daughter of her daughter, might ignite a spark of nostalgic, motherly happiness. I had little understanding at that time of her disease. She did see our baby; there was no spark.

A much improved Bob came to the hospital a few days later and our happy family went home to our two-room third floor apartment. Bob was well again and as instructed by the doctor, washed his hands almost as much as a person with obsessive-compulsive disorder. He had a few days off to help me get adjusted to life as a mommy as well as night life with a newborn. Everything went well until the morning he had to return to work. That's when my panic set in.

"Do you really have to go back to work already?" I whined.

"Yes, honey, I do. Come on, you'll be fine, everything is going great. I'll call you at lunchtime." He smiled, kissed me and left. I looked down at the sleeping little girl and cried. Although my crying was most likely hormonal in part, I remember feeling very frightened and alone. Since I was the first of my friends to embark on this great adventure, I felt I didn't have anyone I could really talk to about the baby. Having the pediatrician's phone number taped to my phone didn't count.

I became increasingly nervous about feeding Colleen; I didn't really know how much milk the baby was getting. She kept falling asleep after only a few minutes of nursing, then waking up very often from hunger. This pattern continued for about two weeks. By the time we went for her first pediatrician visit, she had diarrhea, was not sleeping for any length of time and was crying a lot. He examined the baby, looked at me and smiled. "The baby is healthy and she has gained weight. However, she most likely has diarrhea because you seem to be a nervous wreck which makes your milk inadequate." I stood there *feeling* inadequate; I had on a dress that was not all the way zipped up in the back. The front of me was soaked because I had leaked milk. The doctor, a kind, fatherly type, gave me an understanding look and explained. "Look at yourself. You have to relax. She is fine. Stop nursing and give this sweetheart a bottle!" Here was a simple solution to my first problem as a mom. I learned then it's not a weakness of character to ask for help when you need it. I am sorry I did not tuck that lesson away for future reference.

A bit of luck and a cooperative baby got us through the usual trials and tribulations of parenthood. We moved into a two-bedroom garden apartment with a lovely courtyard. Our neighbors were mostly young couples like us. In the nice weather we would sit in the courtyard, watching our children play, smoking cigarettes and drinking coffee. We had the best of both worlds as mothers of young children;

staying home to care for our children while also being able to have some daily adult conversation. This is a real bonus when it's just you and a two-year-old alone for ten hours (or more when he gets some overtime) until Dad gets home. Any conversation at all with a grown up during the day is better than, "Let's go find your binky and blankie and go night-night. Or, do you want to play with your bow wow woof or your meow kitty or your dig-dig truck?"

About two years after Colleen was born, we decided it was time for her to have a sister or brother. This time, when my nine months of "radiance" were at an end and my hemorrhoids at their worst, my doctor had the good sense to tell me, "Even though Bob is now sure of his way to the hospital, it is still quite a distance from your apartment. It is usually the case that second babies will arrive faster than first babies. Since your first baby came so quickly, how about we admit you to the hospital when I find that the baby is ready? We can induce labor and that would mean none of us would worry that you might not make it to us in time." That was certainly fine with us. Bob thought jokingly about taking some preliminary antibiotics to ward off diseases this time. After all, I did want my husband to visit me in the hospital. The antibiotic idea was voted down by the doctor, though, because you don't take antibiotics until you actually get sick. We packed up Colleen, took her to stay with Bob's parents and his two grandmothers who also lived at their house, to make extra sure she would be spoiled rotten. I was admitted to the hospital early in the morning. In

1972, some hospitals had begun allowing expectant dads into labor and delivery rooms. However, at a recent birth in the hospital where I would be a patient, one dad had become so overwhelmed with emotion upon the birth of his child that he had fainted in the delivery room and fallen, striking his head and breaking his leg. The resultant commotion in the delivery room caused the hospital administration to again put privileges for expectant dads on hold until further notice. The nurses told Bob to go to work and they would call him when our baby was born. I went into labor and about two hours later, Kelly came into our world. The nurses let me call Bob from the delivery room. He had just gotten to his first job at a different hospital, working on a project for the phone company. He turned the car around and drove back to the hospital where his wife and new daughter were waiting, wishing he had ignored the nurse's well-intentioned instructions and stayed nearby in the hospital waiting room.

We continued to thrive as a family in those years. I was happy being a wife and mom. Bob enjoyed his job. We had good friends who we saw on weekends Since most of us had small children, we would take turns entertaining at each others' homes since no one had money for babysitters at that time. At these impromptu gatherings, we would bring our children and they would fall asleep on couches or on the floor in sleeping bags. We would play cards, talk, watch a sports event on TV or play board games. When it got late, we would load the car with sleeping kids and go home. I remember mostly the *good* times of our early family life. We were the parents of two healthy, adorable little girls who continued to thrive under our watchful, loving, constantly learning eyes.

We thoroughly enjoyed our daughters growing years. Each accomplishment, each milestone each adventure was a different experience for them and for us. Since it is true that there are no instruction manuals that come with children, we muddled through many decisions that came along and I am sure we made some that may not have been the best ones. I was a nervous over-protective mother until one of the girl's kindergarten teachers said, "Are you by any chance thinking of getting a part time job in the future?" I did get a part time job about a year later. It took me longer than that to realize what that well-meaning lady meant. She was very wise; my girls needed a bit less minute-by-minute mom management and a little more time figuring things out for themselves and being just kids.

Me, Mom and the Family

My mom continued to work as a secretary while her department went threw many layoffs (from 47 engineers to 4). Then, at age sixty- three, she was asked to take early retirement with a very nice retirement package. They were closing her department and had nowhere to transfer her. I suspect that by that time, her behavior and work performance had changed and they felt she should retire. Retirement was her downfall. She then had nothing to get up for in the morning. I believe that on some days, she started drinking in the morning and did so for most of the day. I spoke to her every day, but did not recognize the problem. I did not have a car in those days, so Bob and I only visited with the baby every Sunday, when she would try to persuade Bob to drink with her at ten a.m. when we arrived. He thought this was a bit early. I tried to make silly excuses for her, but it was just my head-in-the-sand syndrome kicking in, I guess.

Mom was also having pain in her legs and was due to have a test in the hospital one Monday. The Sunday before, the phone rang in our apartment at about nine a.m.

"Honey, can you bring some aspirin over today?" It was Mom. Her voice was tiny, weak and shaky. She knew we were going to look at a house for sale close to her apartment and would be stopping by to see her.

"Mom, what's wrong, did something happen to you?"

"I fell and hit my head and I don't feel good," she muttered softly.

"We'll be right over," I said. "Are you bleeding?"

"No, not now," she answered. I mouthed to Bob to get the girls ready to go.

"Just sit tight," I said, trying to sound calm. I hung up and called my aunt because she had a key to mom's apartment and could get there before we arrived. She went over to make sure Mom did not need an ambulance and was there when we arrived about twenty minutes later. Mom was sitting in her favorite chair, dazed, but conscious. She had a bump on her head with dried blood. Her glasses were broken. At her front door were several empty scotch bottles. I was speechless. The apartment was cluttered and dirty. It was only a week since we had seen her. What was going on here? I felt like a bolt of lightning struck me: *Your mother is really in bad shape and the time has come for you to help her.* I always thought this was the type of person you found on the street in the gutters of New York City. The extent of my denial over the past year or so hit me like a brick; instant guilt and shame kicked in. I called mom's doctor and he recommended bringing her to the hospital for admission. They could do the test on her legs and afterwards we could figure out where to go from there. Where to go from there turned out to be bringing her immediately back to our two-bedroom apartment. She sobered up in the hospital but refused any other treatment. We brought her to our apartment and it was then we began to experience the scope of her disease.

Our daughters were four years and eighteen months old. My mother's doctor thought my mom should not live alone anymore. I too was waking up quickly to the reality of the situation. The doctor had finally seen the severity of her drinking problem through more thorough testing while she was in the hospital after falling and his many conversations with me. Bob and I felt frustrated, but decided to start looking more seriously for a house, bringing mom to live with us. We would move her to our apartment in the meantime and rearrange the very small bedrooms of our duplex apartment to get along the best we could until we found a house. We knew we were headed for all-encompassing changes in our lifestyle. I had no idea at that time of the magnitude and far-reaching effects those changes would have. I felt so grateful and exceptionally lucky to have Bob's support, strength and love during those difficult times. We both grew up in homes where our grandmothers lived with us, so we were both fairly accepting of the concept. In fact, his family had both grandmothers living with them at one time for a few years. Even so, I felt ashamed that I was placing this burden on our young family.

We found a four-bedroom Cape Cod style house in a lovely town with a great neighborhood, and good schools. We moved into our new home and gave mom the largest bedroom on the first floor, across from the bathroom. We took care of closing up mom's apartment, selling some of her furniture and moving the rest into her new room. She went through of all this in a somewhat stunned state, as everything was happening very quickly for her. What we had thought about my mom's future, was now a reality much sooner than we expected. Our little girls seemed a little confused too. First Nana moved into our apartment and their beds had to be moved around, crowding things quite a bit. Then we moved all of their belongings things to a totally new neighborhood and new house.

I was at a loss as to how to help Mom. I was twenty-six years old. I was operating on only basic common sense, compassion and a desire to do the right thing for everyone in my family at the same time. I took her to her doctor for blood pressure checks. She seemed either very agitated and upset or sometimes quiet and subdued. It seemed that she would develop medical problems on a weekly basis, which always needed immediate attention.

"Leanne," I heard from our screened-in porch as I was weeding the garden just outside. The girls were playing in the yard with me.

"What, mom?" I looked up at her. She had her purse in her hand and sounded upset.

"I need you to take me to the doctor, my blood pressure is up." she answered.

"Did you call the doctor's office? Did they tell you to come now?" I asked. I doubted this was the case.

"No, I am just going to walk into the office. They will have to take me."

I tried to reason with her and asked that she let me call to get an emergency appointment, telling her she might have to wait a long time if she just walked in, or they might not be able to see her at all today. I was envisioning having to entertain my four year-old and eighteen-month old in a waiting room for an hour or longer. Maybe the doctor wasn't even there now. She was relentless. I gathered up the girls and we got into the car. They were, of course, not happy that their play had been interrupted on a beautiful summer day. I always had coloring books, crayons and small toys in the car. These "emergency" visits to Mom's doctors had been happening more frequently, so I was prepared. She was seen; indeed her blood pressure was too high and she was given new medication.

This type of behavior went on for about the first six months after we moved into our house. Mom was prescribed a tranquilizer to relax her and lower her blood pressure. This made her sleepy and more depressed. Unbeknownst to me, when I went out, she would order bottles of alcohol from our local drugstore/liquor store that had delivery services. She was secretly drinking. The real nightmare began. When her bottles ran dry, she started on our liquor cabinet. When I noticed a very reduced amount in a bottle when making a drink for myself one evening, I was stunned. I started marking all of the bottles, thinking maybe I was mistaken. I did not want to confront her and make things worse without being certain of what I suspected was a progression of her addiction. It took only a few days of watching the bottle levels go down and down to confirm my worst thoughts.

After breakfast, Mom would take her medication and go back to bed to rest. She took her high blood pressure condition very seriously and the doctor told her rest was important. Since she also was taking Valium, she would doze off sometimes. One morning, I was passing her room and I saw flames shooting up----- the sheets were on fire. She had lit a cigarette while lying in bed and had dozed off. I was suddenly running, shouting, getting her out of bed, getting water, checking on the girls' whereabouts in the house, just beside myself with rage. This near catastrophe did not seem to really faze my mother too much. "Oh," she said, " I'm sorry. I didn't realize." It took all day for my hands to stop shaking.

I monitored her very closely for the next few weeks. One afternoon, I heard a loud crash from her room. She had opened the top drawer of her bureau and pulled it too hard. She fell backward, landing on the floor on her back with the drawer on top of her. She was stunned, but not seriously hurt. I smelled alcohol on her breath.

The confrontation I had known was coming was now at hand. Bob and I had gone over and over the problem. Unfortunately at that time we did not know what resources there were available to us. I hoped that if I gave myself time to calm down, I would again try to "make everything all right" until something like this happened again But, next time might end in tragedy, so I decided not to calm down.

"Mom, you have succeeded in making me a virtual prisoner in my own home by your drinking and by smoking in bed. I calmly stated. "I am afraid to go out without you because I am so afraid you are going to either injure yourself and/or burn down our home. You must stop drinking immediately, or, I will pack your bags and put you out on the sidewalk. That's it. You will not ruin my family! I will get you whatever help you need, but you must stop *now*."

She looked at me with a blank stare, walked over to her chair, lit a cigarette and sat down. I stomped out of her room.

Things were quiet that evening. The next day, I began to truly believe that God had answered my months of prayer. Although Mom didn't say much for a few days, she stopped drinking and never had another drink again, to my knowledge. She never asked for help in recovering, even when I offered to get counseling for her from a doctor or minister.

This began a new part of Mom's story and a new phase of my story. A mother and daughter relationship I never had: a good one. Marie finally took the advice of her doctor and went to see a psychiatrist for help. Within three months, with the help of the proper medication for depression and some therapy sessions, she was making real progress. For the first time, I had a mother who I finally got to know as a woman; a mom I could talk with and relate to.

She woke up to the fact that she had two wonderful granddaughters just waiting for love and attention from her. In time, their wish was granted. They adored their Nana Marie and the feeling was mutual. They would sit with her in her room and play with her parakeet if he was out of the cage. They watched game shows with her. When I was sure she was well enough, I went back to work part-time in a local hospital, knowing she was at home after school for them, which in my mind was the next best thing to me being home.

Because our house was only a few blocks from a main street in town, there were buses running that would take her to the malls. She would go whenever she felt like it and shop or "hang out" with other seniors who enjoyed this pastime. She now felt independent. She did not have to rely on me to drive her everywhere. A group of seniors congregated at a local Woolworths and she made friends there too. She even met a gentleman who drove people to doctor's appointments and airports for a small fee. She joined the Ladies Auxiliary at the hospital where I worked and spent many happy hours volunteering at their café and sewing puppets for the Pediatrics Unit.

The best thing about Mom's recovery was that she and I actually got to know each other. After all, I stopped knowing her when I was eleven years old; she had "gone away" then. Now that she was in her sixties, I had a mother who I loved for herself. We talked, we laughed, we were friends. She listened to anything I said; she was a real "shoulder" for me. She was also a big help to me with the girls and the house. I came to rely on her as never before.

In 1985, mom became physically ill. She collapsed in a local diner, one of her hang outs. I got a call from the police: she was unconscious and they were taking her to the hospital. I got in the car and met the ambulance at the hospital. After many tests, they were still not sure what had caused her to black out. After being home for a few weeks, she then had a seizure, which hospitalized her again. Finally, on a CT Scan, a shadow on her lung was found; a few months later, upon further testing, she was diagnosed with lung cancer. The pulmonologist came to me while I was at work in the hospital and told me the cancer was Stage IV and inoperable. He laid out her options. When I went home to tell her, she told me she did not want any treatment. She was seventy-four, content with her life and did not want to go through any more prodding and poking. I respected her decision. That was in October 1985. She had a wonderful oncologist who understood her choice. He monitored her carefully for changes in her status and medicated her accordingly. As a result of the excellent care she received, she had few disabling symptoms until her last days. Even her spirits remained good. We tried to make that Christmas very special as we thought it would be her last. No one really talked about "it" a lot, being the "let's not talk about serious issues" type of family. My brother was coming east (he was a dairy farmer in Wisconsin) in May or sooner, to see Mom. The doctor had said he would tell me when the end was close in plenty of time so that my brother would have time to get here.

At the same time this was happening, Bob's mom fell seriously ill in February. She had surgery, but complications set in. She remained in the hospital for eight long agonizing weeks and died in April of 1986. Her death was so unexpected; she was only 68 and a very vital spirited, loving part of our family. It was one of the worst times I can remember for the family. Trying to balance care for two critically ill loved ones was something I never wish on anyone We still miss Bob's mom and her lively presence and happy smile.

Hospice volunteers and nurses were now coming to our home a few times weekly to monitor my Mom. She was now using a walker to get to the bathroom because she was very weak Hospice volunteers would sit with her and cook lunch that I would leave for her when I had to work. On the days they did not come and I was working a half day, our daughter Colleen would walk home from school just down the block to fix her lunch and sit with her for a while. She once got in trouble when a teacher saw her coming back to school a bit late one day. When she broke down in tears and told the teacher why she was late, all was forgiven.

While Mom was enduring her last days, she was still smoking heavily. As long as someone was with her to watch her, why shouldn't she? Michelle, one of her steady volunteers, said to me one day, "I have never had a patient dying of lung cancer that still chain smoked!" "Why not?" I asked. "It's a little late to stop." She chuckled, having nothing else to say.

One morning, Mom did not wake up. She was in a coma. I called Hospice and they advised me she would most likely remain like that until all of her bodily systems shut down. I was concerned about fluids and nourishment, but of course at this time, it was unnecessary. Indeed, her systems *were* shutting down. Her life was ending. I stopped working and stayed at home with her. The oncologist had told me about two days earlier to call my brother, which I did. He was leaving as soon as he could to drive east. I was hoping Mom would hold on. She did have one hour where she sat up and was lucid for awhile and, believe it or not wanted a cigarette. I did not give it to her. We hugged, not letting go for a long time and told each other we loved each other many times. She then lay back down and fell asleep. There were no more words. Marie's life had ended.

We called the funeral home right away. Our main concern, was that Mom was out of the house before the girls got home from school. I did not want them to see her carried out of our house in a body bag. My brother and his family were on their way, but did not get to our house before her death. She did know though, before she went into the coma, that he was on his way and I know that comforted her. My brother did arrive and stayed for a week, as he had originally planned. Although he had not been in time to say goodbye, our families had a good visit and our children got re-acquainted.

Wake, funeral, aunts, cousins, brother, all pretty much

a blur. My mom's death was expected. I did feel relieved to see her suffering over. What I did not expect was the crushing rush of emotion rising within me. So much of the past came back to me, making my mind cloudy and out of focus. I was astonished at how upset I was. My mom was very ill. I knew her death was coming for months now. Why was I so thrown by this? The common sense part of me said, "Because she was your mother, you moron." I realized then that no matter how sick, how old, or what the life circumstances are, the death of a parent is very traumatic. As a result, I am thankfully a much more compassionate person. For me, Mom's death stirred up so much of the past, so much that I had tucked away neatly in a far away place. It had suddenly become very vivid to me, both the good and *all* of the bad.

I made an error in judgement at that time in the parenting category with our daughters. I was too intent on getting our daughters back to normal life. By insisting on this and being my controlling self, I did not give them time to grieve. I never really talked to them about how they were feeling and I still regret being so inconsiderate of their feelings. There were previously scheduled milestone events at school coming up the next week; a prom, an overnight class trip. I did not even ask if they wanted to stay home, if they were sad, if they wanted to talk about Nana dying. After all, this was their Nana Marie, who lived with us for thirteen years. After she became a whole person again, they counted on her when I was mean, for extra hugs and all the other reasons grandmothers are so special. They walked by her room where she lay comatose for days, timidly asking me how she was and getting evasive answers from me. Bob had taken over household duties and took care of the girls while I stayed with Mom and slept in the small TV room next to her so I would hear her at night. My mistake was in thinking they were like me, neatly tucking away grief, being strong and carrying on with life.

I see the mother/daughter relationship as one of most complex relationships in all cultures around the globe, throughout time, as evidenced by the vast number of stories and books written about the subject. This is my contribution. Here's to you, Mom. Rest in Peace

SUPER *Boomer*
Daughter
Wife
Mommy
Careerwoman

The Other Side of the Waiting Room -
30 Years as a Medical Support Person

THE TITLES WE ARE GIVEN and/or earn during our careers change over the years. The first job I had after graduation from college was as a secretary. When I returned to work part-time after our oldest daughter started school, I became a medical secretary/assistant in an ophthalmologists' office. This meant I learned to do everything secretarial in a physician's office. In addition, I learned to do anything else the doctor wanted me to do. This included putting patients into exam rooms, prescreening patients with basic vision testing and examining their current eyeglass prescriptions. Since there were many elderly patients, I helped them in any way they needed. The biggest stretch of my abilities was occasionally assisting the doctor with minor office procedures. The entire staff knew how to do "everything," which was the case in most doctors' offices at that time. No one who applied for that type of job questioned this. These were the years before everyone became a specialist, including the employees working in a doctor's office: receptionist, medical assistant, billing specialist, coding specialist and surgical scheduling coordinator.

It turned out that the medical field was something that truly interested me. I was fascinated with the job since it was never boring. Every person and his ailment or circumstance was different. We never knew what could happen on any given day. The ultimate reward was that I helped to make people feel better, if only by talking to them or providing a comforting smile or touch.

After four years in a private physician's office, I felt ready to move onward (and upward) to a job at a local reputable community hospital and got a job as the "secretary to the Director of Rehabilitation Medicine." Wow--I had a really big title now, but was still "just a secretary," as many other hospital professionals referred to us.

Unfortunately, after eight rewarding, happy years working in that department with many dedicated physical therapists, my boss, the director, died suddenly. I was left in career limbo. I continued to work in the physical therapy department, helping the department secretary; she was very happy, but I looked for a transfer because I felt I needed a change. I found one a few months later that looked like it would be a good fit. I interviewed with the Department of Pathology and was offered a job. This would prove to be a big transition. First, it was a new, much larger department. In most hospitals, each department becomes a type of "family" for staff members, so I was anxious to fit in (as usual). Second, I found Surgical Pathology to be fascinating, but a real challenge for my computer literacy. I entered into a brand new world with state-of-the art computer programs that were specialized in laboratory reporting of diagnoses and a computerized dictation system. I would also need to learn a completely different medical terminology vocabulary.

Now, even my title would be more complex. I was *still* a medical secretary, but at Level I because I was new to the department. By reaching certain performance and technical criteria, I could reach higher levels: Medical Secretary, Level II or Medical Secretary, Level III. These represented a fancier nametag, more responsibility and a better salary. For some reason, titles started to take on more and more meaning to many workers in the late eighties and nineties. In reality, though, I felt that they sometimes were not well suited to the actual position held by the employee. Coincidentally, managed care appeared. Remember that phase of healthcare reform? This change in insurance was going to make everything much easier for all, right? We were all were assured that the patient's needs were at the core of whatever changes the hospital made, as they always had been. Tasks were added to many positions because someone had retired and was not replaced. The remaining employees needed to absorb extra work but, of course, that was not to make a difference in anyone's performance, even though they were now expected to do more in the same number of hours. New titles, more important-sounding titles, were given to jobs. Some workers were appeased by the new, corporate-sounding titles and didn't really mind the extra work--at first. Housekeeping was now Environmental Services. The cafeteria staff was called Food and Nutrition Services. A telephone operator was a Telecommunications Representative.

During this period, an opportunity arose for me to take an associate management position. With that, *another* new title would be mine: "Assistant to the Director of Laboratory Services." (I was *still* a secretary). In addition to that official title I would also be the secretary for the five pathologists in surgical pathology, but since you could only have one title, the laboratory one was mine. My responsibilities changed but I felt adequately trained by my predecessor, who retired after 30 years of service.

Then over the next few years, changes and new responsibilities in the original position were gradually added: more monthly statistics, budget plans, inventory control, human resource and payroll problems. Although this is normal in most jobs, I decided I really was not right for these tasks. I missed processing surgical pathology reports, talking to surgeons and their offices, preparing slides for seriously ill patients going for a second opinion and working with medical records for medical conferences. I was feeling more and more that I could not keep up with my responsibilities. I felt as if at 7:00 a.m., I was thrown onto a merry-go-round, which went around faster and faster as the day wore on. Then at about 6:00 p.m., I would be thrown off, some folders were thrown off on top of me so that I could take them home, which I usually did. I gracefully left the hospital after eighteen years.

When I remember the number of talented, dedicated people I worked for and worked with over the years, many stories come to mind. Here are a few memories from my thirty years as a "Medical Administrative Support Person" (That's the latest *title* for my job in the 21st century).

OUR SWEET MARTHA

Martha was a very sweet eighty-five-year-old lady, who was in the hospital recovering from a stroke. She was weak from staying in bed for a long periods when she was first admitted to the hospital (in the eighties, you actually stayed in the hospital until you recovered almost completely). She now was brought down to the Rehabilitation Department Gym for physical therapy: assisted walking, mild strengthening exercises and often, a bit of TLC from the therapist. She was an adorable lady, always happy to talk with us. Martha had been coming daily for about ten days

My office was located just outside of the large gym where the patients were treated. Patients coming from outside the hospital for treatment entered from a separate door into a waiting room outside the gym. I worked for the director of the department but also served as receptionist for therapy patients when my coworker was busy. One day, I was screening a patient who had arrived to see the doctor for some testing. At the same time, one of the therapists was helping. Martha walk past my office door when she suddenly clutched her chest and started to fall to the floor right in front of my office door, groaning softly, gasping for breath. The therapist who had been holding her gently lowered her to the floor as she lost consciousness. "Martha, Martha," the therapist called loudly to her before starting CPR. "Get help," he said, looking up at me, with a controlled, calm voice.

I knew that I had to get the doctor, but his office door was about fifty feet away. The only way I could get there was to leap over Martha and the therapist. (Thank God for my dance background.)

Unfortunately, Martha had died instantly of a heart attack. Emergency measures taken at the time did not help her. As she laid in front of my office door, waiting for a stretcher to take her to the morgue, the patient who was due to see the doctor for his appointment came up to within a foot of Martha. He looked directly at me and asked me if I could fill out his disability form because it was very important that he have it that day. The therapist, the doctor and I turned to look at the patient, who seemed oblivious to the crisis going on around him. He was only focused on his forms and his problem. The event that had just occurred seemed to have no effect on him. The three of us were speechless. The doctor took the man by the arm calmly and professionally and led him into his office. The therapist took a deep breath. Shaking his head, he went to fill out the hospital forms necessary in this type of incident and call Martha's attending physician. I took the patient's disability form, went into my office, sat down and tried my best to stop my hand from shaking as I wiped away a tear from my eye and filled out the moron's form.

THE WAITING GAME

The first indication that people in the waiting room are getting impatient is that they have stopped reading magazines, started looking at their watches more frequently and are sighing deeply. The tapping of nails on a magazine or the arm of the chair is the next signal of frustration.

We all know the frustration of having to wait in a doctor's office. After all, we think, our time is valuable too. This is true. However, physicians deal with daily unpredictability of human beings, sick and well. There is sometimes very little that can be done to prevent delays in a doctor's arrival.

One day, our doctor was very late and we were beginning to become concerned. He had not called, which was unusual. Karen, at the desk, said, "People are beginning to send very angry looks my way. What do you think is keeping the doctor?" A tap, tap, tap was heard on the reception desk glass window.

A young woman said, "Miss, how much longer will the doctor be? I made this appointment specifically so that I could leave by 3:00 p.m." in a tone that was not friendly.

"How come that doctor isn't here yet? Don't he know we're waiting?"

"Hey, sweetheart, why is it taking so long? I want to get home in time for my TV show."

"I'm sorry, ma'am, but the doctor has been delayed in surgery. He is on his way and should be here soon." It is always best to be honest with the patients. If they get really upset, we try to explain, "If you were having a serious surgical emergency, we would hope he would be available for you." That stops most people from saying anything further.

"I'm at a complete loss," snipped Lori, our nurse. She was counting the number of seats left in the waiting room. Only two were left. It was 2:00 p.m. and the 1:00 patients were still out there waiting. She told us later she figured she had to do something really crazy to lighten the tension. We saw her open the door to the waiting room filled with aggravated patients. She stood up straight with head held high, put on her biggest smile and start to sing, "When You're Happy and You Know It, Clap Your Hands." She continued singing to an astounded room full of patients. The rest of us in the office were too stunned to do anything for a moment. Finally, we broke into falling-off-the-chair laughter. The patients could not help but laugh, and it did break the tension. A guardian angel must have been watching too and decided to help the situation a bit--the doctor arrived a few moments later. As always, he managed to appease the patients. He did wonder why most of the patients were not complaining and some even had a little grin on their faces when he went in to the exam rooms to see them. All was well again in surgical land. Under normal circumstances, our nurse was a big favorite with the patients. Now, they truly appreciated how special she was.

THE JOGGING PATHOLOGIST

Early morning surgeries sometimes required the presence of a pathologist in the operating room to take a sample and test the tissue for cancer cells. The doctors in the department would alternate this responsibility. Doctors are people too, with their own idiosyncrasies and habits.

One staff member was a physical fitness enthusiast. He liked to jog in the morning. Next to the hospital was a school with a running track. The doctor usually arrived before he needed to be on call, ran a few miles and then return to his office to do paperwork and be available if the operating room needed him. By this time, I was usually in the office to take the operating room calls. Before that time, he would use his pager. This was before cell phones were in use.

One particular morning, he was a little late arriving. I was in the office enjoying the quiet. He came into the pathology department and said, "I am going over to the school track to jog. I will take my pager, so if the operating room calls for me, you can page me. If the pager doesn't work that far away, you can just yell out the window for me."

I tried to keep my facial expression normal and not reflect what I was thinking. At first I thought he was joking. He was not. I knew the pager wouldn't work that far outside the hospital. Leaning out a hospital window and screaming about one-eighth of a mile did not appeal to me either. I did not think he would hear me since between the hospital and the school track was a very busy parking lot. I tried tactfully to explain why I did not think this would be neither appropriate, nor effective. The doctor, however, was not one to be dissuaded from what he wanted. Off he went.

Murphy's Law being in effect that day, the phone rang about ten minutes later. It was the operating room and they did indeed need a pathologist to consult. I punched the doctor's pager number into the telephone but of course, he did not answer. I went into a part of the lab that I thought would be closest to the track, opened the window and screamed--to no avail. Everyone in the parking lot in front of that window first stared and then got a good laugh, along with the people behind me in the lab who knew what was happening. Realizing that time was of the essence now, I ran down the hall, went out the nearest exit and hustled as quickly as I could to the track. (I was not a physical fitness enthusiast and I still smoked at that time.) When I got close to where the doctor was running, I called that he was needed in the operating room. I could hardly speak because I was so out of breath. He looked at me with a somewhat startled, puzzled expression on his face and said, "Why didn't you just page me?"

This was just one more responsibility not written into my job description with this title, "Assistant to the Clinical Director of Laboratories." As most people who work in the medical profession know, you will do anything necessary at any moment to help when needed without blinking an eye.

There are too many more stories to be told by me here and there are a great many hospital workers across the country who could tell their own. Real life, human stories are what make working in the medical profession so worthwhile, sometimes sad, but stimulating, interesting and rewarding most of the time.

Current Cacophonies
or
Things that Go Blip and Bleep

WHILE CLEANING THE HOUSE ONE sunny spring day, I heard the buzz of my clothes dryer signaling the end of a cycle. Then my microwave bell tolled, telling me that the meat I was defrosting for dinner was ready. Simultaneously, my husband's beeper vibrated itself off the credenza onto the floor. About one minute later, the fax machine in his office signaled an incoming message. I was momentarily at a loss--which bell do I answer first? I felt like I was in the Twilight Zone. Beeps, buzzes, bells and blips--all attached to modern contrivances that keep us running on a never-slowing treadmill of modern living (my treadmill also emits a few sounds of its own).

It seems to me that as technology advances, the array

of devices "necessary" to our modern lifestyle increases with each blink of an eye. This seems especially true for a resistant-to-change, technologically-challenged baby boomer like me. I decided to define and make an official count of all the "blips and bleeps" which were an important part of my day.

The invasion of my brain begins each day with two alarm clocks; one next to the bed and one on the dresser across the room. The clock on the dresser of course does not turn off until I am in an upright position and manually shut it off. The clock next to the bed has snooze control so when I lie back down in bed after remaining upright for about thirty seconds, I can be awakened again and again until I am convinced that I really do need to remain awake for a prolonged period of time. Then I dutifully stumble to the treadmill (unless I can think of a good excuse--like it's Tuesday--not to exercise). I set the speed and amount of time desired. The bell goes off when the allotted time is over, unless of course I cheat and shut it down.

Okay: shower, dress, off to work. The workplace is a veritable Mecca of signals. Think for a moment of how well-trained the modern human brain is by all of the audio signals in a typical office environment. We can be reading, looking out the window or talking on the phone. But the intrusive noise of a machine will interrupt what we are doing and we will note it in our brain. It is possible to ignore it for a moment and return to what we were doing, but it did invade our thought processes for that instant. I was becoming enthralled with the challenge of this careful enumeration.

1. Turn on copy machine—*Beep*
2. Turn on the computer--*Beep*
3. Login with password-- *Blip*
4. There are 6 e-mail messages for me--my "Notify" *blip* interrupts.
5. Fax: *Bell* for incoming fax goes off.
6. *Beep* signals end of document sent
7. When sending a fax--beep when document has been sent through.
8. The granddaddy of all blips is heard when a paper jam occurs; open door of copier--
9. Blinking lights and blips to tell you where the paper jam is located.
10. Another *beeping tone* when all is well and the copier has "recovered."
11. Dictation/Transcription equipment: (This is a Biggie): *Beep* after input of every document number (one person can do up to fifty or sixty documents per day) At the end of each dictation:—12: *Beep* The main retrieval station for assigning dictation: input code to assign.
13. Beep. Forward to next screen to view remaining documents—14. Loud ring if dictations ended.
15. Morning meeting: During the meeting, three people's *watch alarms* and 16. two *beepers* went off. Watch alarms- time for meds? Beepers— time to call your honey?
17. Telephone: Thirteen lines - One *soft ring* for an in-house call
18. *Double (louder ring)* for a call from the outside.

19. It is noted that 70 percent of outgoing calls bring us no human contact—there are many *beeps* bringing you to an extension or voicemail.
20. At the end of voicemail--BEEEEP.

At the time I first noted this curious phenomena, my office was in a laboratory where many highly technical instruments processed various tissues and specimens twenty-four hours per day, making multiple beeps and blips.

We are also treated to necessary *fire alarm drills* --very loud. *Door alarm*--when some fool opens the door that is clearly marked ---

"DO NOT EXIT-EMERGENCY ONLY- -*ALARM* WILL SOUND.!

I numbered only the routine noises of the everyday machines in use. Multiply these by a normal eight-hour office day and there are a lot of blips and bleeps goin' on here.

Workday is done. I head home for some peace and quiet. Hopefully, the only noises will be the soft melodious meow of my hungry cat. That's not to be. There are three messages on my answering machine. There's a loud *blip* between each message and a lengthy *beeeep* when I erase them. Then I need to reset the temperature control on our thermostat, which beeps at each degree I raise or lower it to; then. . .

Sorry, I lost count.

The Weekend Wives' Club

THE PARTING:

It's 6:00 a.m. on a Monday morning in a quiet New Jersey suburban community. Families start their day. Kids are off to school. Commuters begin their trek to the local train or bus station. The usual routine in *our* house on a Monday morning is somewhat unique. It goes like this: "Bye honey, see you on Friday. Take care of yourself. I love you."

My husband's commute was a long one. He left our house on most Monday mornings and arrived home on Friday night. Instead of driving a car or taking a train or bus to the office, he let a pilot do the navigating to a major U.S. city where his current project was in progress. These week-long trips (and occasionally two-week long trips) became part of our lifestyle from approximately 1988 to 2001. My husband was one of thousands in America whose career demanded extensive travel.

Because I now had extra time on my hands, I began to wonder about other wives living this unorthodox version of married life. I did some informal polling over the years e.g., reading, talking to friends, chatting with strange women after eavesdropping on supermarkets lines, I discovered that there was a growing population of married couples in America who patterned their marriages to fit their careers.

THE ABSENT SPOUSE SYNDROME

When we married, my husband and I repeated "'til death do us part" at the altar. Never in my wildest dreams did I anticipate, "til the *company* do us part"! Would our marriage become a feature in the <u>Ladies Home Journal</u> monthly feature *"Can This Marriage Be Saved"*? Would we end up a statistic in some divorce study about traveling spouses?

My diagnosis for the malady causally related to corporate life in America was the Absent Spouse Syndrome, not found in any medical books. This disease affects wives, husbands, children and other family members. The outcome of this chronic syndrome can be computed like a math equation: number of years traveling + state of marriage before traveling began + personalities of the couple involved = OUTCOME. Personality may be the biggest part of the equation, I thought. It takes an ability to adjust and maintain a certain amount of independence that perhaps the wife was not used to previously (as in my case). It ranks in the same category as any long distance romance you may have tried to maintain. Where did that usually end up? Now you're married and there are usually children you both love, so you must be very flexible and try very hard to keep your marriage strong. Sadly, some marriages cannot not survive. My husband and I are one of the truly lucky couples. We also tried hard.

THE SENSE OF SELF

The women I spoke with had children of various ages and some had careers of their own. I noted that although there were personality differences, common feelings of anger or resentment about this unusual lifestyle would crop up in conversation. Sometimes these feelings can be misplaced and become focused on the absent spouse. It's human nature to blame someone else for our bad feelings. Talking with other wives led me to another interesting conclusion: women who had a healthy sense of self were better able to cope with having an absent spouse. Being your own person besides being part of a couple, lends itself to easier adjustment. These women already had a feeling of independence vital to surviving on their own both practically and emotionally.

A friend whose husband has traveled internationally for many years told me, "We've moved to so many different countries that I've had to make friends quickly, but mostly I rely on myself. It has made me much more independent and has actually helped me to find who I really am, not just 'Donald's wife.' "

In my case, developing my sense of independence was challenging. I did not realize the reliance I had had on traditional divisions of household labor. I now had to take out the garbage and the recycling, arrange for car maintenance, and manage dozens of other tasks which my husband had always taken care of. I learned such useful life skills as what to do when the toilet overflows, how to handle home repair scheduling and knowing what questions to ask of mechanics.

CAN WE TALK?

Absence did not mean total isolation. Frequent communication was the most important coping tool for our absent spouse lifestyle.

Because my husband was not at home every day, it was easy for me to forget events to tell him about important to our family or our home. I sometimes jotted down things I wanted to remember to tell him, even the small problems I didn't expect immediate "fixes" for from 2,000 miles away. He still needed and wanted to know about them. Otherwise, if I did not keep him up-to-date during our nightly conversations, he might return home to an unwelcome surprise.

An acquaintance of mine told me that her husband arrived home on a Friday night, tired from traveling. He saw a pile of ashes and debris in the back yard where the utility shed had been. It probably would have been better if he had already been aware of this household catastrophe, rather than being greeted at the door with, "Oh, by the way honey, the backyard shed caught fire on Tuesday; a small explosion--but thank God, no one was hurt!"

Of course, there was sometimes a flip side to this newfound independence. I managed all week long and learned to do things my own way, perhaps not *his* way, just a different way, and usually with good results.

"Hi, honey, how's everything?" my husband said brightly, calling from Dallas. "Well," I said, "Kelly just ran in from the porch screaming that there is a GIANT wasp on the porch and ran up to her room. I'm just about to go out and spray it with Wasp Stopper."

"Make sure you don't aim the spray through the screen. That bug spray will kill the hedge. It's professional strength and really meant for nests," he warned. "Can't you use a fly swatter to kill the wasp?"

Since I was never too adroit with a fly swatter, I knew I would only succeed in getting the wasp angry, encouraging an attack. I opted for the spray, waited until the wasp was in the upper corner of the porch and was therefore able to salvage the hedges, making our porch again safe for habitation while preserving our lovely backyard environment. I handled this minor crisis my way, but took his good advice as part of the solution. However, despite being able to manage, I always missed his problem solving abilities in household dilemmas-- always logical and sometimes innovative. Most of my solutions were of the quick-fix nature.

A UNIQUE SOCIAL SCENE

What makes the absent spouse situation amusingly unique is that during the period my husband traveled, I remained still happily married. Our friends could not "fix me up" for an evening. I remained in a kind of marital limbo, not divorced, single, or widowed. Whereas I certainly would not go out with another man, most of our social life when Bob was at home did revolve around married couples. Most weekend wives socialized through organizational activities such as adult education classes, church activities, and book clubs.

ALONE VS. LONELY

Despite making best efforts at distraction, sometimes the loneliness can be overwhelming. For a long time, I prided myself on categorizing my situation as being *alone*, not *lonely*. There *is* a difference. I learned that there is an advantage being happy spending some time alone and I always enjoyed my alone time. But, I later found that there is no shame in admitting loneliness in this type of marriage--there is good reason. Those lonely times are real, but if you make the most of your time *most* of the time, you can be content.

Sometimes however, I found myself in an "is-this-any-way-to-have-a-marriage? mood, missing my husband more than usual. That made me very cranky, a feeling which can sometimes turn ugly for unsuspecting souls. I remember a telemarketing call during one of those evenings. I don't recall what she was selling, but it was 9:30 p.m., long past the time I thought appropriate to be to be making a sales pitch. I decided to tell the telemarketer this. "Oh, she said, is there a better time for me to call you?" she sweetly asked.

"Well, how about you give me your home phone number, and I'll call you about 10:00 p.m. on your night off and see how you like it." Not a very nice way to direct my feelings of frustration. I did end up apologizing--just before I hung up on her.

I did none of those things most other weekend wives do with church organizations, classes or book clubs, which was probably a big mistake on my part because I kept to myself *too* much. I started writing, worked more, watched more movies and read a lot. I also started drinking too much.

THE "COUNT YOUR BLESSINGS" EXERCISE

When I was feeling overwhelmed or had the "poor me" feeling, I repeated the following: "I am still married to a loving husband. I am in my own home and I have family, our daughters and my cats. My husband is in a motel room with his work and the TV as his companion; he is eating too much restaurant food and working too many hours."

This little pep talk I used when I was lonely worked most of the time. I was able to accept the situation and move on.

As time went on, however, sometimes the little demon who was taking more and more control sitting on my shoulder would say, "Poor you, poor you, *pour* you a drink."

I had some rough years on a personal level during the last few years Bob was away. I actually liked being alone more and more but began to drink more and more. I was still perfectly happy because I didn't think there was a problem (another indication that there *was* a problem). Our oldest daughter, who lived at home was thinking of getting her own place. A contributing reason was, she told me, "I can't stand to watch you do this to yourself any longer." In November of 1993, I finally got help and after years of a painful, tedious walk down a sometimes rocky road, I became renewed, healthy and happy again. Bob was so supportive; he was and always is my strength, even at a distance. He did not know the scope of the problem early on, but that didn't matter; he was and is my cheerleader. We are still happily married; our girls are married with their own families and doing well.

HOMECOMING

After my husband had been traveling for about thirteen years, we developed a routine and a certain acceptance of this lifestyle. Then, another big change occurred due to corporation reorganization. He decided "no more" and retired from the corporation.

"Hooray," I thought. "We'll be like a normal family unit again!" Bob is home now, working for a different company because after about a year-and-a-half, he found retirement was unfulfilling. The difference is, he leaves home each morning and returns in the evening. We prepared for this lifestyle change with joy. A positive attitude was again the key (also, staying out of each other's way around the house). We escaped the pages of <u>Ladies Home Journal's</u> feature, *"Can This Marriage Be Saved?"* The only statistical report in which we may show up is, *"Number of Married Baby Boomers that are Still Married "* in <u>U.S.A Today</u> or <u>AARP Bulletin.</u>

Would I marry my husband all over again if I knew this situation would become a part of our lives? You betcha!

The Fall of the
Princess from the
Ivory Tower

Good Reason on any Given Day

The sun came up.

I had a bad day at work.

The landscaper didn't show up.

I had a really good day at work.

The weather is awful.

I got a run in my stocking.

The cat spit up a hairball on the carpet.

I did the wash yesterday. Time to celebrate.

The sunset is beautiful. I'll sit on the patio with a cocktail
and watch.

I had a bad hair day.

There's a full moon.

My favorite TV show is a rerun.

THOSE SWEET ELIXIRS SERVED AS my barrier against guilt over inexplicable feelings of unhappiness when I was leading such a wonderfully privileged life. When you drink until you become totally numb, feelings go away; eventually you crave the anesthetic feeling that alcohol can provide 24/7.

My list shows how ridiculous excuses can become. Whether alcoholic or not, people sometimes feel the need to justify things they do or choices they make.

The bottom line is that I drank because I am an alcoholic. Alcoholics don't need a reason, but always feel there should be one, in case anyone asks. People occasionally ask someone in their life who they feel has a "drinking problem," "Why do you have to drink so much?" When I was actively drinking, I would respond, "Why do you have to breathe so much?"

Sarcasm aside, the comparison is an accurate one. It is virtually impossible for a person who is not an alcoholic to understand what it is like to have their life completely controlled by the desire for alcohol. The need to have a drink (and believe me, I never had *a* drink in my life) takes over your complete being; you are its slave. Even when you sober up for a few days because your body needs to dry out a bit, once you are feeling a bit better physically, you cannot wait to starting drinking ASAP. Usually, at a certain point, you are definitely not having fun anymore, but you need the alcohol to survive.

Having described here how I felt when I was actively alcoholic, I still managed somehow to keep a job and performed it well. Keeping the fact that my life was a wreck deeply hidden from most people progressively became more difficult. I didn't have friends and my family knew something was wrong but did not know the full scope; my necessary controlled periods were a practiced skill that most alcoholics develop. But I was only kidding who?

Circling the Drain

My eyes open very s-l-o-w-l-y, one at a time. The pain in my head is so intense I am hoping that when both eyes are fully open, I will find I am awakening from a bad dream. Actually, I am hoping I will just not wake up at all. Then I would never have to feel like this and go through this pain day after day, over and over, because I now have no control at all over my drinking. After a few minutes of consciousness, I realize that is not the case today, or any of the days of my recent past. This is because the night before, I enjoyed a six-pack of beer as an hors d'oeuvre followed by many vodkas as my entrée. My appetite then disappeared and I did not have anything to eat last night that could be called dinner.

My bedside clock says 7:00 a.m. It is time to get up, shower, make myself presentable and go to work. I work very hard to get to the hospital every day, where I have a responsible position in a large clinical department in a hospital. No matter how much my head is pounding, how much my hands shake or how queasy my stomach is feeling, I get there. I feel a need to consistently function with the superwoman persona of wife/mommy/careerwoman/I can do-it-all superbly, which I strive to maintain at all costs. So after showering, I paste concealer under my eyes and put drops into my eyes to reduce the redness. Then I take the strongest painkillers I have on hand. I look in the mirror with a half-baked smile and announce to whomever it is I am seeing there, "On with the show!"

Driving to work, every morning, the voice reprimands me, very loud, very clear. "What the hell are you doing to yourself? If you keep this up, you are going to ruin the beautiful life you have and perhaps kill yourself with alcohol. Living first hand with your mother's alcoholism was not enough for you to see what a destructive path you are traveling? Isn't the effect alcoholism has had on your family life strong enough to put a big red stop sign in front of you?"

I answer the voice every day as well. "I know, you're right, I promise I won't do this again to myself. I will stop drinking *today* because I hate feeling so ill, debilitated and remorseful each morning. I hate stopping at different liquor stores on my way home because I am afraid I will be labeled a 'drunk' if I am a repeat customer too often in one store. I hate having to remember every Thursday to count how many beers are gone from the refrigerator so I can be sure to replace the exact amount (just in case my husband is counting) when he comes home Friday from his business trip(yes, the paranoia is setting in). I am tired of opening a can of Diet Coke, pouring half down the drain and filling it up with rum so that I can still drink constantly when our daughter is home from college or our other daughter is visiting. I hate hanging onto that can at all costs; if I put it down, one of them might want to take a sip of my "Coke." I hate feeling it is a pre-requisite before a social event that I have several strong drinks so that I feel relaxed and comfortable with myself in order to be sociable and to fit in. I am ashamed that I must write down which friend or relative I call to have deep, meaningful, nostalgic conversations with some evenings so I can remember who I spoke to the next morning. During the final months of my drinking, I can no longer read my own handwriting the next day, so even that "trick" doesn't work anymore.

"Click" goes the off button for this tape that has played in my head for perhaps the past 240 or so days. I pull into parking lot at the hospital, resolute, naive, a bit happier, forgetting that this is the 240th time I have made this promise to myself.

After a lunch of fat and carbohydrates to relieve the queasiness in my stomach, I feel marginally better and take my next dose of painkillers for my nagging headache. By 3:00, I am feeling on the verge of okay. On the drive home, the daily morning self-loathing lecture and goal-oriented promises do not even float through my mind. The only obsession weighing on my mind now is pulling out of the liquor store parking lot as fast as possible, driving home, parking in the driveway, getting the mail from the mailbox, unlocking the door. *I am feeling fine now. No need to give up having a few drinks after work.* I pull into the driveway and get out with my supplies. I practically sprint to the door, salivating. I can taste that first one, only minutes away now. I use my key, drop the mail on the table. I do not even take off my coat. I make a mad dash to the refrigerator and open my first wonderful, frosty beer. Instant relief and relaxation takes an insidious hold of me. I am home, I am safe, I can let down, the mask is off, I am me. I then take off my coat, greet the cat warmly and sort through the mail while finishing my first beer and lighting a cigarette. The next five beers (my hors' d'oeuvres of a sort) go down even better. I have to finish all six. Of course, by then, there is no appetite for food. The rest of the night is devoted to other drinks of choice until bedtime. If loneliness gets the best of me, after talking to my husband about our day and what's going on here at home, I call the Alcoholics Anonymous Hot Line to chat with someone with whom I can share this unspeakable secret. They talk to me and are understanding and try their best to be helpful. I periodically promise to help myself, then thank them profusely (people pleaser that I am). Then I hang up and have another drink, toasting the wonderful, kind people of AA.

This was my life on and off during the last 2-3 years of my alcohol abuse, although the last eight months, as described, were the worst. I tried to stop by myself. I tried to drink only wine. I tried to drink only on the weekends (this was the most difficult since I was usually alone during the week and after all, "no one would know").

I was always very controlled then, because my husband was home, we were busy with family or friends. If we went out with friends, I would have a few drinks before and just a few when we were out, so I did okay. I tried to drink water in between drinks. I tried all the tricks alcoholics try to convince themselves that they may have a teensy little problem, but are definitely NOT alcoholics. I registered for several different adult courses, praying to God that if I had something to look forward to after work, something to keep me busy, this might help distract me from my obsession with alcohol. Inevitably, I found some excuse to quit, because COME ON, that silly course was just interfering too much with my drinking time. I isolated more and more, it was so much easier, you see. My memory was getting so bad that in one dance class, I could not remember which step came next unless the teacher was right in front of us demonstrating the steps.

At one point, my husband tried to talk to me about my drinking. We were out to dinner on a Friday evening. We always looked forward to our Friday evenings together when he returned from a business trip. We would have a nice meal and catch up on our weekly activities at work and talk about what was going on with our girls' lives. One evening, he told me that our daughters had expressed their concern to him that I had been drinking heavily for quite some time. He also thought that when he called each night, he noticed I had often been slurring my words. Our daughters reported to him that when he was away, I often seemed to be drunk when they came to visit or when they would call me later in the evenings. He said he was worried and wanted me to tell him if something was wrong. I calmly responded by reminding him that our daughters frequently put a bit too much drama into many situations and that yes, I did have a few drinks at night but was also usually very tired after work, so maybe that's why I sounded a little "off." I congratulated myself for being calm, cool and collected through this confrontation, but I knew that perhaps my jig was up. I had mixed feelings of guilt, fear and relief. Unfortunately, those feelings left me as quickly as they came. The drinking actually got worse.

There is one thing that I always knew for sure, as an active drunk or in recovery. I was always an alcoholic, although not starting to badly progress until my 30's. My husband's traveling came after I started drinking heavily. In no way shape or form does a circumstance like a traveling spouse *cause* someone to become an alcoholic. It may provide more of an opportunity for drinking without being sneaky, but it does not cause the disease. No one held me down and poured alcohol down my throat. My husband's traveling had no bearing on my disease; and now, through education, I believe alcoholism is just that—a disease.

After another year or so of misery, my inevitable downward spiral was complete. My blood pressure was sky rocketing and my blood work was showing abnormalities in liver functions. I became sick and tired of being sick and tired. On Halloween night 1993 around midnight, long after the last trick or treater had gone home, I had my last drink. I fell asleep (passed out) on the couch. I woke up the next morning with a horrific migraine headache. I called my office and told them I would not be in that day, because I was ill. My next call was to the Alcoholics Anonymous Hot Line, not just to chat this time but to find out when and where there was a meeting I could attend. I went to my first AA meeting that evening. It was the most important fifteen-minute drive I would ever take.

Bottom

Wind me up, make me go
To and Fro, To and Fro

Yes, I'll do it, don't say no
To and fro, To and Fro

Losing touch, no more "glow"
To and Fro, To and Fro

Don't know me, <u>Don't want to know</u>
To and Fro, To and Fro

Better for all if I go...............
To and Fro, To and Fro....................

The Calling

An Angel called to me by name
At first light one beautiful morn
"Come to me," this angel whispered low,
" be free, be free, be free. . ."

A light, so blinding, glowing, lovingly inviting
So mysterious - - - beckoning my lowly soul,
"Come to me" the Angel uttered again,
" you'll be free, be free, be free. . ."

Longing for peace, I entertained
answering her tempting call.
I could, if not for all eternity my soul
would languish in that depth too far.
" 'Tis too soon" my mortal being did retort.
"I've more to do and more to be on earth
before I join with those loved, but gone."

My Angel smiled (a wondrous sight)
Gave blessings to me and mine.
"I'll see you in awhile dear one;
your earthly presence will cease.
Then peace will be within your grasp. . .you'll
be free, be free, be free…"

Leanne Garrett Flanagan

This Alcoholic's Dream

To be immersed in a sea of booze once again. . . .
　　to swim in that sea and lap up vast quantities of alcohol.
To quell the constant haunting, whirling thoughts swirling
　　in my brain, like a surging tide.
Oh the blessed numbness I once knew would be welcome,
　　even for only a brief time.

"Don't drink, go to meetings" says that nagging voice inside
　　my head.
To that I want to shout "fuck you! you smug little angel.
　　To bend it's golden halo into a long straw
　　　　and suck vast amounts of 100% proof nectar.
To wallow in a divine anesthetic daydream of nobler times

To have no ill effect from this raucous scene---
　　this is my ultimate delusion.
That my actions cause no hurt as in past years.
　　But I know that I can only dream of such a life,
　　　　or death will claim my being for its own.

Facets

The facets of me are many, you see
Some talented, some mysterious, inane.
All are a part of me, some are the heart of me,
all twisted links in my chain.

There's Hilary Humorous, Wanda the Wit
and Suzy Sarcastic as well.
Cindy the Cynic and Ballbuster Bev
They think verbal stings and jabs are swell.

There's Alice the Addict, you name it she's in.
She'll embrace each drink with such fervor.
That twist in her gene leaves her less than serene,
so now no one ever will serve her.

Doris the Doormat, once the dominant one,
the ultimate, pleaser, do-gooder.
Oh yes, sure, right away, whatever you say.
What me, Doris? Say No? Never ever!

Sally Selfish-me, me, me-that's all that you hear.
Then two others who add to her tune,
They're Wendy the Whiner and Penelope Pris.
It's a good time *they* manage to ruin.

Dancing Debbie, my favorite, fulfilling my dreams.
Mary Musical belts out those tunes.
Chris Creative, she writes for family and friends,
But publishing—just a pipedream?

In comes Nancy Neurotic to stir all of "us" up,
Franny Fearful chimes in close behind.
It makes for one hell of a life after all,
I try hard to hold onto my mind.

If Alice the Addict had not interfered,
My psyche would be more stable.
Alas, healing and peace should have sooner arrived
and combined to be Marvelous Mabel !

These intense little chicks, I am starting to think
Take a few traits -----they're not sooo bad.
For I'd be Betsy Boring if some weren't outpouring
It's more <u>fun</u> to be just a bit mad!!!

My Other Demon, Depression

WHEN IN THE THROES OF full blown alcoholism, I struggled with the age-old dilemma, " which came first, the chicken or the egg?" In my case, it was, "which came first, booze or the depression?" I thought if I could get rid of the depression, I could stop drinking. But alcohol is a depressant. So then, if I could stop drinking, maybe I could get rid of the depression. Thankfully, I finally did the right thing. I got rid of the booze, then sought help for the depression. However this incipient recurrent disease of depression returned with full force after I got help for alcoholism. I believe this other demon of mine is also biological and in my case lingers in my genes, too.

BEFORE MEDICATION:

I want to be left alone most of the time. Social contact with anyone is a really painful effort. I manage to get myself to work and function, although my concentration is poor. The effort to take a shower and dress is, in and of itself, a monumental annoyance for me. Then again, I think if I don't take a shower, I will be offensive to others. Can't everyone just leave me alone?

No—I have to act nice and normal even though it's very hard for me. I put on my *as if* mask and I wear it more and more, which is exhausting. Being with sad, apathetic, depressed people is very uncomfortable. I know this firsthand from living with my mother in those years when she was so severely depressed. I consistently tried to bring a smile or feeling of happiness to her without success, not understanding the disease at that time. So at all times, I must act *as if* there is not a thing in the world wrong with me. After all, look at me: I have a great life, a great family, no financial worries, two wonderful daughters, a loving, supportive husband. I am sober and working hard at my recovery. I do not want my family to be upset or think they are making me unhappy because they are not. There is no rhyme or reason to these feelings. I am just so sad and feel so hopeless. Can't everyone just leave me alone?

I have this "I am going to cry any minute" feeling every ten minutes and it is getting pretty lame. I rarely cry for any reason, so what is happening now? Everything is so hazy and unclear for me. If everyone would just leave me alone, maybe I would be okay. Why do I have to talk to anyone, except at work? The little angel on my shoulder that usually talks to me seems to be on sabbatical. I feel like I am only living mainly to just endure life. Suicide is not an option for me because I believe it is the greatest sin. God created us and we cannot destroy what he has created out of love; this is my belief. If only I could pray for his guidance. I cannot even get myself motivated to do that! I wish everyone would just leave me alone.

My favorite relaxation is to read and I can't even do that. I just can't focus on the words. I feel sad and mournful *all* of the time. I want to be left alone.

"What's the matter?" Bob says to me when he comes home from a business trip. How can I explain this to him? (I really just want to be left alone.)

"Nothing hon, everything is good," I reply, changing the subject quickly. He of course can tell when I feel down, but I really trying hard not to let on the scope of my hopelessness. It is almost impossible for me to find words to describe it so that anyone would understand.

One of my greatest fears is that I will turn out to be like my mother, alcoholic and severely depressed. But, oh my God, it is happening. My little angel suddenly returns from her sabbatical or wherever she was. She reminds me in no uncertain terms that yes, I may have inherited two nasty, destructive genes from Mom, but I have already gotten help for alcohol abuse and I am doing a good job at recovering. "Please leave me alone," I plead with her. I thought I wanted her support, but now I want to crawl into a hole and die. Do I really know what I want?

"Now, listen you whiny little moron!" she is now shouting and I am covering my ears. "Stop this stubborn independent streak of yours. You could not stop drinking on your own. What makes you think this depression is going to just go away on its own? Get to a therapist NOW. Deal with this NOW."

I go to sleep for twelve or fifteen hours or more, get up, eat a pint of ice cream and seven or eight or ten cookies. Then, I walk past a mirror, inadvertently glance at my reflection and nearly jump out of my skin. I am ready. I need more help. NOW.

I call my doctor and make an appointment for a physical. He walks into the exam room, looks at my chart, looks up at me and says, "How are you feeling?" I start to cry.

He says, "Get dressed. Forget the physical, come into my office."

I do; we talk at length. He prescribes an antidepressant, explains every detail of the drug and how it works. He also discussed the disease of depression, biochemistry of the brain, serotonin and neurotransmitters. I find this all difficult to follow and I am losing focus, which he knows, but he also gives me the name of a good therapist, some literature and a hug.

AFTER MEDICATION:

After three weeks, the medication has worked a small miracle. I feel like I now am actually living and functioning almost normally, genuinely happy when appropriate, sad when appropriate, mostly just like a normal person (well, almost).

Therapy, on the other hand, causes me a lot of emotional stress and pain, dredging up some past issues which needed to be brought out in order to move on with a recovery program. I later realized it was very necessary to the overall process of change I needed go through within myself and in my thinking if I want to stay sober the rest of my life, which I do. The most important thing therapy taught me was a self awareness of what had happened and how I can help myself. More importantly, I learned that a huge step is learning to forgive yourself. A lot of insight was gained during those sessions that contributes to my current state of happiness and sense of self-worth. My healing was progressing nicely *with help.*

OOPS

Three years later, I decided all on my own (I'm a big girl now) that I was doing so well, that I did not need these medications anymore. I was mostly likely cured and did not need them. It couldn't be a good idea to take these type of pills for such a long time, right?

I did very well, I thought. I actually was almost euphoric for about three months. No problems. Look at me. I'm fine. What do those doctors know? This is great. Little by little, in subtle, small ways, I started down the steps to renew my relationship with my recurrent enemy, the demon, depression. I stopped going to AA meetings, making excuse after excuse. I stopped putting on music when I got into my car. I stopped reading. I put off shopping, cleaning, and most other normal life activities along with things I enjoyed doing. I was reminded by my loving husband that I was not quite myself lately and that maybe I should go back to see my doctor. I called, made an appointment and entered her office a bit nervously. I humbly (because I knew I had screwed up) told her what was going on. In her very tactful, professional and caring manner, essentially reamed me out for doing such a stupid, potentially dangerous thing on my own. "Just think of depression as a disease like diabetes. You *must* take this medication to keep your disease under control; to survive and remain well. If you prefer, you can think of these medications like vitamins to stay healthy. Either way, you must take the meds every day for your entire life."

Since that day, I have not stopped taking my medications. When a thought of maybe taking less or stopping one of the medications entirely enters my brain, I think of that very wise, caring doctor's words and call or visit her and we discuss a change or reduction, if warranted. This works. The moral of this story is: If you need it, take it. . . . .Don't worry, be happy..

THE AWAKENING

or

It's a Better Life in the

NOT-SO-FAST LANE

Watch That First Step---It's Amazing

IMAGINE WALKING INTO A ROOM of about fifty strangers, feeling alone, afraid, desperate, confused and maybe physically ill. Twenty-five or so of those strangers turn around and watch you walk through the door, as if you're not already self-conscious enough. Six or seven people get up, walk towards you. You wonder if you are in the right place. Or maybe they will ask you to leave. One or two woman greet you with a "Hi, how are you? Is this your first meeting? My name is Janet, or Nan, or Sue or whatever." One woman about your age says, "Please come in and sit with me. I can probably tell you how you're feeling right now. (I'm thinking, no you can't). Please believe me, it's okay to feel scared, very confused, tense and wanting a drink---stop me when I get one wrong," she continued. "But I will tell you with 100% certainty that the majority of us here felt the same way for exactly the same reason you do. Stick around after the meeting and we will give you our phone numbers in case you want to call us when you get home tonight or any other time you need to talk. We will also answer your questions and give you some literature you can read when you're calmer."

I took a very deep breath, immediately feeling more comfortable. Wow, could this lady be any nicer? I had no idea what to expect next. All I knew was that I felt that she really did understand how I was feeling. What I was experiencing was total, instant acceptance, no judgments made, no questions asked. For that moment, I felt safe. I felt hope. I fit in.

I naively thought this seemed like it would be easy once I accepted group support. My journey back to health and sobriety was anything but easy. I thought I would learn the program, go through it and "graduate." As the fog in my head and heart cleared, it became evident to me that I had lost an identity because of my drinking. It slowly dawned on me that in order to become healthy again and stay that way, I must change my thinking and behavior or else I would eventually start losing the few people and things I cared about, ending up in that same self-destructive Hell again. I felt a little like this was the end of the worst performance of my life and the curtain had finally come down. Now with a lot more rehearsal and many drastic revisions, I would be given a new opening and I could enjoy a long run of goodness.

The next ninety days, there were a lot of meetings. There was a lot of emotional pain. There was a lot of talk,

talk, talk with other women who had been through this withdrawal and rebuilding of themselves as a person. That is really what I needed to strive toward as I healed—to find the part of me that I'd lost. The one who used to like theater, reading, music, sewing, socializing. The one who never used to lie to people for convenience sake. The one who was reliable, honest, thoughtful with fun in her heart.

I had cravings for alcohol often and at weird times. I dreamt about alcohol, too. I sometimes dreamed I was drunk (but having a great time). I thought, "Oh no, just when I was starting to feel better, I am drinking again." When I woke up in a sweat, I was so relieved it turned out this was just a dream.

I realized and accepted that going to meetings was a lifetime commitment. There is no graduation from addiction; there is no diploma or certification. There is no cure. I believe alcoholism is a disease and there are many clinical studies which document this, although some still disagree.

That first step - - the admission that I needed help from an objective outside source was the hardest task I have ever undertaken in my life. The admission that I could not independently fix a problem was totally new for me. That something so destructive was controlling me. That I had tried to stop drinking; tried to "fix" myself and could not. That I felt lost, unhappy, inadequate as a child of God, a failure as a mother and wife, and worse, guilty because I knew I really had nothing to be unhappy about compared to most other people in the world. That I could only escape these stupid, ghastly, insane feelings by drinking enough to be anesthetized, so much so that my body needed that feeling to be what my warped thinking judged as happy.

When I found other people who felt as I did and who had faced their problems, I became hopeful. When I saw that many were in fact recovering and leading happy, fulfilled lives for a prolonged period, the feeling of hope overtook the helpless feelings I had for quite some time.

The pleasures I had stored away for so long were now within my reach again.

Celebration

I *see* with eyes God gave me.
I hear the sounds sent by Him.
I smell and taste the wonders of nature's bounty
through His generosity.
I feel the richness of my spirit through
these gifts God has bestowed.

The depths of my soul and mind are blessed
I love
I feel
I give
I am

For there are miles of beach to walk.
To feel the sun on my face, wind in my hair,
the surf and sand between my toes.
Happiness is holding on to His presence everywhere.

The woman I celebrate is at peace with GOD,
a miracle born of the gift of *like*.
Education of my *self* shows me the way.
Support and love shows me the light,
now burning so bright.

Adversity will not snuff out this flame
nor send me back to the glass.
For knowledge of my self-worth inspires freedom
from despair in the bottomless bottle I once knew.
It allows my soul to soar with joy,
in simplicity, serenity, in faith.

The Virgin Commute

Should I drop these pages of opportunity into the recycling? Should I finally do what I constantly talk about and take the plunge into the world of writers aspiring to publish? I will never know how difficult the writing world is unless I try to make connections. If I want to take my writing further than "Lee's Lousy Limericks" and pitch the work sitting in my notebooks, I will fill out this registration form and go to this writing seminar in Manhattan.

THIS IS A SAMPLING OF the motivational speech I gave myself that morning. The seminar was at Marymount College in Manhattan. It consisted of panels and discussions concerning writing in all genres, along with how to pursue publishing, hire an agent, the pitfalls and tips. There would be guest speakers and opportunities for questions and discussions with published writers. And there would be lunch.

Scanning the contents of the brochure, I again experienced the same anxiety that I had before the brochure originally went into the recycling bin. Going to this workshop in Manhattan meant I would have to travel by bus, train *or*, God forbid, *drive* into *THE CITY*. As a lifelong suburbanite, commuting to New York solo was like taking off in a spaceship to Mars, alone, with no map on a cloudy night and no stars to guide me. Would I make it safely to this large, unexplored territory, this scarred jungle of humanity with crime-ridden streets? YES, my adrenaline started pumping. I would conquer *the commute.*

Registration mailed, I researched bus and train routes. At one point, I panicked and started calling limousine services. That idea was quickly diffused when I discovered the rates for a fifteen-mile journey (I may be afraid, but I'm also cheap). I consulted people I knew who were familiar with New York City, some veteran daily commuters. Their matter-of-fact suggestions were mind boggling to the novice commuter. One well-meaning friend told me to take a bus, then two subways. She then went into great detail about which subway train at which station, where to make the switch and the various safeguards to take to make sure I wasn't attacked, since I was new at subway riding. I stopped listening at the word "subway." A news headline developed in my brain, "Mumbling Woman Found After Wandering for Three Days in the NYC Subway."

Ultimately, I decided to take the bus to Port Authority and spring for the cost of a taxi to my workshop site. NJ Transit was most helpful in getting me onto the right bus leaving not far from my home, bound for the Port Authority Terminal. My plans were now complete for my solo adventure. I felt excited, brave and nervous, like a little kid before the first time walking to school on his own.

Bright sun and blue sky greeted me on the day of the seminar. This matched my mood as I eagerly awaited my bus. I looked forward to gaining a new sense of belonging. Today, I was one of millions of commuters, a common camp of people enduring bad weather and unscheduled mishaps, mechanical difficulties and traffic delays, all to get to their jobs. Quickly, I discovered that not one of those campers on the bus was a "happy camper." First, I made sure the bus I boarded was indeed going to the Port Authority (one can never be too sure). The bus driver immediately labeled me a virgin commuter as he loudly proclaimed, "Yes lady, you have the right bus to New York City." I made my way down the aisle of the bus, holding on as we jerked to a start. I was prepared to greet the few people that were staring at the big red "V" for virgin on my forehead and say "good morning." You know, that normal courteous pleasantry many of us were taught growing up. My first wake up call came. *No one* smiled or spoke. In fact, most never even lifted their heads as new riders boarded at each stop. The Pope could have boarded the bus and I doubt anyone would have noticed. I felt like I was getting on a bus of the living dead, being transported to nowhere.

Secondly, I realized was that most people wanted to be left alone in order to sleep or read, but certainly not to make idle conversation with a seat mate. I realized that since buses have double seats, the further along on the route we went, there was less chance for a having a seat to oneself. I picked the least harmless-looking young woman and took my seat. She moved her work papers slightly and "allowed" me to sit (gee, thanks honey). I too took out the writing that I had brought with me in my briefcase so that I would look very professional (when in Rome). The silent commute continued.

The journey was uneventful; none of the nightmarish traffic delays I so often hear about on my radio in the morning. Near the end of our ride, I mustered up the courage to ask the woman next to me her advice on purchasing a return ticket. I felt I had to break the bus etiquette code of silence for my own welfare, because of course I was already worried about losing my sense of direction on my trip home. I hoped that no one would glare at me, or worse, for my breach of conduct.

I got off my bus at the Port Authority Terminal, undaunted by the apathetic attitude of the bus passengers. I felt exhilarated at being on my own in The Big Apple and the thought of mingling with fellow writers at a seminar with well-known published writers as speakers was already inspiring.

Plenty of time remained before the seminar started, so I headed for a coffee shop in the crowded Port Authority terminal. I was met with the same blank, dispassionate faces at the terminal. I felt like a very tiny fish in a vast sea of humanity. Certainly, no one was interested in my reasons for being there, but the writer in me hungered to ask people where they were from and what their jobs were, or their reasons for coming to New York that day. I reasoned that if people would just talk to me, I could get at least two or three essays or material for a few stories or poems. However, the majority of faces I looked into had a vacant "I just want to get where I'm going" look or a preoccupied "I'm in my own world with my own stuff goin' on" look. I decided this was not the time or place to gather material. Thinking about this afterward, I did scold myself, realizing that a different writer would have been more aggressive and attempted to stop people and interview them anyway, having no fear of repercussion. But at that time, I wanted to "belong" to this commuting club, so I would follow their rules as I imagined them, written like graffiti in a subway station:

Rules of the Commute:

1. No smiling or cordiality of any kind.
2. Maintain an attitude of total indifference and passiveness.
3. Do not react to anything seen or heard during your trip either by facial expression or body language. This includes the humorous or the horrible.

The next leg of my journey involved finding a cab to take me across town, or downtown, or somewhere in town. That proved to be easier than anticipated, since

I was still at the Port Authority Terminal where an abundance of cabs awaited me. I was really lucky here. I found a pleasant cabby, a fairly safe driver who spoke understandable English. I gave him the address of the seminar, Marymount College, and asked him if he knew where it was. Here again I showed my naiveté. This was a New York City taxi driver. It was his job to know where everything was and if not, he had maps and resources. He gave me a look and we pulled away from the curb at about forty miles an hour. As we sped towards my destination, weaving in and out of early morning rush hour traffic, I noticed that the people crowding the sidewalks all maintained a similar demeanor to those of the bus passengers and coffee shop patrons. The scene reminded me of a futuristic movie where people are treated like herds of cattle, moved from place to place with expressionless faces. I wanted to scream out the window of my cab, "WAKE UP, NEW YORK. IT'S A NEW DAY, ACT ALIVE!"

I was feeling more and more like a naïve, stupid hick. While I do not pretend to be a worldly sophisticate, I was not prepared to accept the degree of passivity I was experiencing. I decided I did not want to be a member of this club if it meant adopting this apathetic persona.

The seminar turned out to be excellent (lunch was delicious too). This made up for the earlier disappointment in my morning commute. I met many people who wrote on different levels, in different genres and styles, for various reasons, having different personalities and eccentricities. Elmore Leonard was the featured speaker of the day. He spoke with eloquence and humor about his books, his methods and his many experiences during his fascinating, lucrative career. He had begun just like all of us who sit at our computers in the wee hours of the morning, doubting that what we write could ever be appreciated by anyone else. His career had skyrocketed to where he now has his own research assistants and other business guidance galore. I felt inspired as a writer and left with new hope for future projects.

Making my way back to the Port Authority Terminal in the late afternoon, I reflected on the day. Boarding the bus to make my return trip, I found a seat and gratefully sank down into it amidst other commuters. I too was feeling tired and anxious to get home. I looked around the bus at the other tired faces and thought, "Hey, I actually feel a bit more like I belong." I easily understood the reason for no communication or joviality on my return trip. We all had a common goal, to reach *home* as quickly as possible.

What began as an advertisement in my mailbox became a learning experience I will never forget. Among the things I deduced from this trip, there are a few I'll share: I am basically happier as a suburban naive hick chick. I do not ever want to be a regular commuter into New York City, no matter how good the salary. Taking that first step of intercity travel solo however, was definitely worthwhile. Even if things turned out badly, there is always something to be learned - - my mother was right - - one's character is strengthened by it. By far, the best thing I discovered was that "getting there" is *always* part of the fun in life's journey.

Increasing Fits of Happiness

The turbulence, drama and emotional upheavals of my life are in my past. Therefore, you may want to conclude that the remainder of my years will be hum drum and ordinary. Not so. From my point of view, the years have gotten and will continue to get better and better. From the turbulence, drama and emotional upheaval, I have learned self-awareness, which I believe is a key tool in life. It reminds me to be honest, tolerant, to reach out to others, most importantly for me, not stay within myself. I now know I cannot please all of the people all of the time

During my recovery, I realized my job and I were not suited anymore, no matter how much I valued my loyalty to the hospital. After leaving there, I had two other jobs that turned out to be disasters. I realized that because I had previously been in a management position, it was very difficult to go backwards and no longer have any authority. A former co-worker asked me if I was interested in doing some medical typing at home for her boss. I started to do that and enjoyed it. By getting in touch with contacts I had made in past years, I collected a few more clients and developed a small typing business, which continues to do well today. I make less money, offset by the enjoyment of the work, flexibility and variation of the work I do. I go to one client's office part time and do the rest of my work at home. This gets me up, dressed nicely and out of the house a few days during the week. So now, I have the best of both worlds in my work. The bonus of this job is that I work with a small group of ladies that I not only work with; I laugh with them, cry with them, share family milestones with them, share the good and bad times with them and eat chocolate with them. We are a family. I believe that God's intervention in my recovery by even entering my work world. Another fit of happiness.

My family life only gets better year by year. I think Bob and I have gotten closer as the years have gone by. We got through the years with my mom's illness. When she recovered, and then became physically ill, we handled that as well, the physical aspect difficult in a different way. His quiet strength and support has always been my anchor. We have deep pride in the accomplishments of both daughters. They were typical teenage girls and I always refer jokingly to their teenage years as "The War Years". Overall, we were lucky; no arrests or other real catastrophes (that we know of anyway). Lots of happiness here.

Our marriage has changed, as I think is probably a

normal passage in life. Our love for each other has matured. We are happy with each other, even if sometimes silent in each other's company; content to watch TV or read or do crosswords together. We love to travel whenever we can and have had some wonderful trips to far off places. We take great pleasure in our beach days, lying on the beach, people watching. We are still very happy to see each other at the end of every day. A *big* fit of increased happiness.

The beach days are not always quiet however. Two weeks during each summer, we do not go alone to the beach. We venture to a part of the Jersey Shore where there is no boardwalk, no concession stands, only dunes and beach. We rent a house and bring our daughters and their husbands, our absolutely adorable highly intelligent grandchildren and Bob's dad. Each day, we carry beach chairs, umbrellas, sand toys, towels, coolers, blankets and beach games, becoming exhausted by the time we walk over the dunes and get to the ocean. We take half an hour setting up, the children go into the water, play in the sand, throw sand, the youngest eats sand, we eat lunch, ride the waves, splash by the edge of the water, argue about taking a nap (some days they do, some days they don't). They play catch or fly kites or bury dad in the sand. At times, one of the younger ones is crying because he is tired and does not like the sand on his body and the baby is running into the ocean with his mother chasing him screaming, "Wait, wait, stop running!" It is often chaotic and it is the highlight of our summer. After we get back to the house, the children are showered and usually watch a video before dinner. We sit around with some cucumber sandwiches, chips and salsa relaxed and happy, laughing about the events of our beach day. It is family. It is another happy fit in my increasing fits of happiness.

I reached 60 in the year 2007. I am a certified baby boomer and proud of it. Many articles have been written for and about women of our generation. I surmise that many women (without being an alcoholic or suffering from chronic depression) feel as I do, that the age of 50 to 60 is perhaps the best time of your life because you are finally comfortable with who you are and hopefully even happy with who you have become. I certainly am. For most women who are married, the children are grown and perhaps married. Maybe you have adorable, highly intelligent grandchildren as we do, who you can help to care for in some way. You are now a bit freer to do what you want, even if you are still working as some of us are, either by choice or because we need to. There are so many options open to us nowadays; volunteering is a growing choice for many, with an increasing variety of opportunities from which to choose. When I retire, I hope to take on a part time volunteer job; something to do with reading or music for children or maybe the elderly, or both. I am overdue to start giving back. Here is another type of happiness that will bring fulfillment as well as help to others.

I see increasing fits of happiness in every aspect of my life now. I realize I am not addressing the craziness in our global situation or the economic ups and downs. I do watch the news. I do see the breakdown of common decency and the disregard for human life that goes on in the world. I pray a lot. I am not an activist; nor am I Little Miss Sunshine. I am somewhere in between. I still battle with depression. The difference now is I can accept that I have limits, but am inspired to do what I can, one day at a time. I will start on the local level to set an example and hope the younger generation will be able to turn things around for the world. One can only hope . . . and pray.

Meanwhile, I will continue to enjoy my INCREASING FITS OF HAPPINESS

Letter to a Friend

My Dearest Friend,

This time is a reflective one for me. Lying prone on my couch, I am recovering from a surgical procedure, forced to do nothing but rest. You already know my health will be restored. I need only time to stay quiet, nourish my body and heal. Anyway, I have been looking back to the past during the last few days and looking forward as well. Overall, life has been a joyous journey for me so far. Having you as a friend has enhanced the journey. You and I have been close friends for so many years. In fact, I can't seem to remember when we weren't talking, laughing, consulting, disagreeing, crying or celebrating.

Growing up, you showed me that the best way to be happy was to be a caring, responsible person, to value life, be tolerant, charitable, strong, cheerful and most importantly have faith. Oh yes and to laugh at myself!

162

When we strolled together for a morning walk, we always saw so much wonder in nature, sharing enjoyment of wildflowers in the park, waves at the beach, seagulls swooping down over the dunes. Do you remember the frogs we saw actually playing leap frog on the lily pads in a pond near our favorite lake? Our friendship truly radiates warmth, like the sun on a field of flowers. I feel so very grateful for our special relationship.

Of course, like most relationships, our friendship has weathered some stormy times, as you well know. The best part though, is that afterwards, we were always able to laugh over those disagreements and debates about the state of the world and our role in it. I recall telling you once that I could no longer be your friend because your views and activities alarmed me so much! I had difficulty understanding how and why people hurt each other, fought wars and were so hateful to their fellow man that God so loved. How could you think the way you do and still be my friend? Of course I was happier when things were going my way, it's the nature of my psyche! However, it always seems as though when I give up my strong will, things work out for the best.

And so, when I gave up that will you again became my confidante, my helpmate and comfort in my darkest hours through those difficult years I had. When my soul was spiraling into the depths of uncertainty and it seemed that I would never be able to ascend to any level of spirituality ever again, you did not abandon me, but sent help through your faithful servants here. I am grateful for your patience with me. Progress, not perfection is one of our favorite sayings. You certainly seem to have the knack of keeping me on the right track now! I sometimes feel I am on the taking end of our relationship too often. I am constantly trying to give back to you as true friends do. As Walter Winchell once wrote, "A friend is one who walks in when the rest of the world walks out!"

So here's to us—hats off, cheers, hurray and hallelujah! I promise always to take time from each day to think about the connection we have, savor the special moments and to renew my pledge to remain true to you always. For it is my fervent hope dear friend, that when my weary body bids its final farewell to this beautiful earth, that you will open your loving, forgiving arms and receive my soul into Heaven for eternity.

Your faithful friend and loving servant,
Leanne

C h a n g e s

Nature offers a miraculous gift of artistry to us,
   Painting an array of new colors; a feast for our eyes every
     few months.
Weather changes set the stage for another season,
     another page in another chapter of our lives.

Each season takes a different form and with it, although perhaps
     unaware, so do we all.
   Metamorphosis most dramatic is the winter into spring,
The green we see out our window is no longer snow covered
     evergreens, but green grass peeking through the
     melting snow.

This change from winter to spring lets us reach out,
   aspire to a new awakening after the hibernation of frozen
     winter months.
Warmer winds and brighter sun change our mood.
   Smiles replace the winter pallor on our faces,
     we are energized!!

As bursts of color explode in our gardens and in the trees,
   we listen to the sweet songs of the birds,
having renewed hope for the days ahead reveling in new life
     and new growth in the midst of the chaotic events of the
     world.

Warm to sultry, summer comes.
     Our spirit shouts, "Step back! Enough! Take a break!"
   Sweltering bodies seek water, a respite by the sea
     or days in cool summer air of mountain lakes.

Riding the crest of ocean waves, we take the ride down
  into Fall as nature changes the landscape yet again,
from bright summer colors to rich, warm gold and orange
    hues; a unique crispness to the air that refreshes after
    smoldering August days.

We've had our rest we, start afresh; back to work,
    back to school;
Like a new fall school outfit, a new outlook after the
    complacent mindset of the summer.
Fall signals us to pick up the pace once again
    as cooler temperatures overtake the warm summer sun.

Winter comes once again. The cold gradually creeps into our
    bones.
Grey skies prevail, turning moisture into delicate flakes of
    slippery white.
A clean blanket covering the ground making the world pure for
    awhile; hearty folk bear the cold for winter sport.

We choose mid winter to celebrate holidays,
    seeing exquisite delight in children's faces.
Family ties sometimes rekindled like a newly stoked fire.
    Abundant goodies cover our tables, a joyous time.

The changes within ourselves are like the seasons
    Some subtle, some drastic, some exhilarating, some
      overwhelming.
Throughout our lives. . .
    it is the only constant.

Longevity

So much talk, so many articles, TV shows and self-help books on living longer. We are inundated with information designed to enthrall us with the idea that we should look forward to living to the age of one hundred. We are told the catch is we must work at getting to our nineties by staying healthy through preventative steps and finding any serious problem early. This time-consuming, money-draining trend has certainly caught on. Just ask the pharmaceutical companies, the people who make vitamin supplements, the exercise equipment manufacturers, the gyms and of course, the plastic surgeons.

I imagine God smiling down on us, watching all of this and thinking, "You silly humans, it's a good thing I love you all, for you can sometimes be so flighty and misguided. Death is inevitable. You can fight all you want but when I put your number into the computer, that's it, no matter how many protein shakes you drink."

Personally, I give anyone who wants to live to be one hundred a "good luck and God bless." For myself, I have no wish to live to be very old. I would like to have another good ten or fifteen. I have extended that estimate recently only because I now have adorable, highly intelligent grandchildren and would like to see them grow and thrive. I really think I will have had enough of the world as I know it by then. I am very happy now. I have everything I want. I look forward to a wonderful retirement for Bob and me.

In this regard however, there is conflict between my wish and Bob's thought on the matter of death. His longstanding mandate to me is that he dies first. When he first told me this about fifteen years ago, I said, "Who says?" His comeback was, "It's in the marriage license. You must not have read the fine print at the bottom. Didn't you see it?"

I was laughing by then. "Of course not, there is no such clause! Why do you want to die first anyway?" I asked. I was very curious. It seemed obvious to me that he must have given this some thought.

He was ready. "Because it is a statistically proven fact and I believe it is true, that in general, women deal better over time with the loss of their spouse than men do. They adjust better and faster. I don't think I could handle it and don't want to handle it. I saw what my father went through when my mother died."

My adorable husband often reminds me of this

"clause" in our marriage license and we laugh about it every time. I am sure God is also laughing. I do, however, agree with this theory. Most married women spend their lives managing households, nurturing children and often handling jobs outside the home.

Women can always find things to do because we have always had so many things to do. It is easier for us to keep busy, so time passes and helps the healing process when something bad happens. We usually have a few outside interests, even though they may have been dormant for a few years. We are also more likely to have the desire to socialize. Men usually rely on their wives to keep their social calendar and therefore, if they lose their spouse, they are at a loss as to what to do for a rewarding life outside of their work.

I plan to enjoy my happiness for however long I have here on earth. I also plan to try to feel as well as I have since I began recovery from two insidious diseases. Will I spend a lot of time and money trying to be younger than my years? No. New technology is replacing existing technology faster than I can keep up. I will spend time learning about communications technology, which affords me enjoyment. If medical technology will give me an end to a painful situation in the next few years, then I will take advantage. I am old–age resistant, not stupid.

I also have the other usual reasons for not wanting to live to an unusually old age. Like most people, I do not want to rely on my children. They are caring children. I know they would do what they could to keep me comfortable. I still don't want to have to rely on them.

Leanne Garrett Flanagan

I don't want to be helpless in any way. I don't want to be in a nursing home or any facility resembling one. I had an aunt who I was very close to. I admitted her to a nursing facility when she was eighty-nine. I visited often at various times during the day and evening to be sure all went well with her care. It was a good nursing facility by the standards in our state. It was still awful. I could almost see inside some of the patients' minds, especially the ones who were seriously disabled and could not communicate well. I looked into their eyes and imagined what they might be thinking: "What's wrong with all of you? Don't you see my dignity is being stripped away here, my last bit of independence being taken from me? Don't you see my life, my money, my strength is being drained slowly, ounce by ounce, day by day? When my family does visit they look at me with kindness and love, not knowing what to do to ease my pain and my loneliness. Don't they know that I often wonder too when God will take me? I wish I knew how to reach them, to tell them not to worry. Don't they know that I am already dead inside?"

So I would rather quit while I'm ahead, as the old adage says. If I develop a terminal disease ten or fifteen years from now, I seriously question whether I would do anything radical to treat it. People give me an incredulous look when I say that. I tell these people, maybe God's finger is ready to push the delete button next to my name on the computer.

My ideal old lady's life would be to spend my remaining years in a cottage by the sea with dunes along the path. It would be a hideaway of perfection for Bob and me. There would be a picture window looking out onto the surf and from our sun-drenched deck we could watch the rolling tide. After all, time means nothing to the waves. Inside, we would have all the simple, comfy stuff. Books, music, a flat screen, hang-on-the wall TV with a remote so the Bob that could watch sports, and I could watch movies. There would be a cozy kitchen, two recliners and a flowery, puffy couch for naps. The kids and grandkids would visit during the summers (when we invite them), bringing good steaks. Oh yes, there would also be a dock for fishing and crabbing.

In the sunset of our lives, who can tell, maybe we might both fall deeply asleep, our bodies listless and relaxed while watching the sun fall slowly, glowing radiantly, going down, down, gradually creeping down amid blazing tones of brilliant yellows, pinks and orange gently falling beneath the horizon. . .God willing, our lives going peacefully down with the sun . . .together.

The End

When gone from this life (it's been fun here on earth),
how will people remember me?
The girl, the woman, a person of worth—
the dancer, the writer, a lady of mirth?

Or will they just list the usual stuff
the daughter, the wife, the mother.
Fulfilling--the best part of life, that may be
But I really don't think it's enough.

So, after any speeches, toasts or boo hoo,
I'd prefer that in my obit,
That the person *I* was is recorded there too.
Then more happily in Heaven I'd sit. . .that's it.

From a Collection of Lee's Lousy Limericks"
2010

Acknowledgements:

My HEARTFELT THANKS TO MY editor, Marcia Trahan, for her expertise, sincerity, honesty and guidance. To my brother Curt, who filled in some memory blanks, thank you. To Margie Gelbwasser, a talented instructor whose critique was a huge help. For their incredibly patient and professional help, thanks to Bob DeGroff and Mary White along with the production staff at Author House. For giving me the first draft suggestions, grammar help, opinions and advice I desperately needed along the way, Helga Burke—you're the best. To Jenny for her story about patients, thanks. To Joy for her encouragement to pursue the dream. My thanks to Pinnacle Press for patiently resolving my imaging dilemma so beautifully. To my lifelong friend Dolores for her "poll" of perspective readers, thanks for giving me some faith in my writing. Thanks to Rayne Debski for her published writer's viewpoint and survey efforts which validated my own thoughts. Thanks to those in the special club I proudly belong to that sustain me one day at a time. To my terrific daughters who always encourage me, I love you.

About the Author

A NATIVE "JERSEY GIRL", LEANNE WAS born, raised, educated and still resides in Northern New Jersey. A passion for literature, classical music, dance and musical comedy directed her activities throughout childhood, adolescence and college years at Rider University. She took a 30-year "sabbatical" (experiencing real life, raising a family, a career in healthcare). College courses in creative writing, many seminars and workshops encouraged her to begin the long journey towards publication. In renewing her passion for writing she writes light, tongue-in cheek observations of life in American suburban society, limericks and poetry. She resides in a Northern New Jersey suburb of New York City with her husband of 42 years and their cat Sophie.

Look toward retirement, her hope is to share experience, strength and hope of recovery through speaking and writing. The dream is that those who need help getting through just one more day / hour / minute can read something in a blog or article to give them a laugh and the strength they need.